LIFE of BRIAN

in

BLACK & WHITE

Fifty years following Newcastle United

by Brian Hall

with cartoons by Paul Burke

NORTHERN WRITERS

First published December 2007
Northern Writers
"Wor Hoos"
28 Cockton Hill Road
Bishop Auckland
County Durham DL14 6AH
www.northernwriters.co.uk
www.writersinc.biz

British Library Cataloguing in Publication Data
A catalogue for this book is available from the
British Library.

ISBN 978-0-9553869-2-3

Typeset in 10/12pt Garamond
Typesetting and origination, printed and bound
by Lintons Printers Ltd, Beechburn, Crook, Co
Durham DL15 8RA
www.lintons-printers.co.uk

FOR THE FANS

Contents

Cartoons

Introduction

This is the story of one Newcastle United fan from birth to the present day.

Brian's first visit to Gallowgate in the early Sixties saw the team crash out of the FA Cup against non-league Bedford Town. It was the start of a journey in which he experienced nightmares and dreams, also felt by the rest of the NUFC tribe. There have been highs and more lows, but it all remains worthwhile.

Along the way, Brian has made friends with many of his fellow fans. Some of them are in this book, but all members of the tribe have their own tales to tell. They are United in a common bond – supporting a unique football institution. Once you join the tribe you are in it for life. It is, as they say, part of the culture.

Enjoy the read, the incidents and the characters in this Black & White journey. Whatever happens, Keep the Faith!

Brian Hall
Heaton, Newcastle upon Tyne
December 2007

Chapter One

Reflections

Brian was looking at notes on his life with Newcastle United, and thinking of the many incidents and characters he had met in his five decades following this unique institution. It was a Monday morning. A Barclaycard bill landed through his Heaton front door, and for once he was pleased to see it. It confirmed that the money had gone out for his season ticket. His pleasure lasted only a second, as he realised that, due to an administrative cock-up, the club had taken out an extra £900 or so from the account. The next day was dominated by rumours of a takeover bid for United.

This led to frantic telephone calls amongst Brian's Mag mates, and occasional sights of some of them buying the Financial Times for further information. They normally bought a pink paper, but that was of course the Football Pink. Wednesday saw the new hope for another New Dawn, Michael Owen, crumble in excruciating pain in the early minutes of an Ingerland football match in the World Cup. Brian and most of his group had one major priority in that World Cup – not to see Owen crumble in excruciating pain.

Meanwhile, Newcastle's new manager, Glenn Roeder was trapped inside Warwick University, on FA instructions, being forced to study on how to become a manager. This allegedly involved, amongst other things, a lecture from a certain Mr Sam Allardyce.

None of the above was untypical in life with NUFC. The Evening Chronicle, which gives a blow-by-blow account of daily activity at St James Park, uses the slogan "The Week That Woz." Brian often wonders how many times that slogan has been applied, and could have been applied over the last half century. True, this club does have dour, dull, soulless spells, but they never seem to last long before some NorthEastEnders drama breaks out, whether on or off the pitch.

Sacking managers at the beginning of a season, potential glory collapsing into disaster, fans whose moods range from blind optimism to despair within the space of a weekend, demonstrations against the Board, the club dominating tabloid front page headlines for activities unrelated to football, are all par for the course.

The list is endless for a set of supporters who live and breathe United. Some dream of major domestic silverware which the club have not brought to them for over fifty years, others just accept that they will never see a big trophy anyway. The latter group includes Barry, one of the Felling lads, and Claire, daughter of Brian. Barry said this in his early twenties a few years ago, and Claire is only 17.

This book is no detailed research of every United game and season, full of facts and figures. Far better writers have done that. Rather it is a story of the Black & White Life of Brian, with memories of life following the Mags. It's a story of the incidents, the pain, the joy, and the downright bizarre events which he and his group of friends and acquaintances have experienced. It reflects the stubborn loyalty of these people.

Above all this book is a tribute to the men and women, boys and girls, who support this club with such intense passion and pride. A small set of them are in this book. Obviously, thousands upon thousands are not. There is only one reason why Newcastle United can claim to be a big club. Their empty trophy cabinet wipes out any such statement based upon success on the pitch. Rather, they can only make the assertion on the base of the passion, loyalty, and the sheer numbers of their following. As Sir Alex Ferguson once said, they deserve better, although he never extended that sympathy to the pitch when his team played them.

Chapter Two

No choice but the Mags

The Black & White Life of Brian began on 29th
August 1957 in a back bedroom on a council
house estate at Penshaw near Shiney Row, a
small, bustling Durham pit village. Years later, the
area was occupied by Sunderland Council,
although Brian and most others, particularly the
local Mags, refuse to recognise the annexation.
His family is of Northumbrian and Scottish origin,
with some distant Irish link way back in the past,
an origin shared by many in this region. Naturally,
he knew little of his fate as a Mag. The United
tribe were in fact a minority in the village, but it
should be emphasised at the outset that they were
never oppressed. Just a glance at some of the
characters from Shiney Row in this Life of Brian
will confirm why that never happened.

       The baby was blissfully unaware that at
the time of his conception back in January 1957,
Newcastle were suffering a 6-1 defeat at the hands
of Manchester United, with only the heroic Jackie
Milburn scoring for the unborn lad's future team.
In the decades ahead, Brian would become only
too aware when Manchester United were giving
United a good hiding. The first season of the
young Brian's life saw the team in a decent eighth
position in September, plunging out of the Cup to
lowly opposition in the winter – this would
become a familiar activity – and narrowly

avoiding relegation. The Mags managed to win only six home games.

However, two days after his birth, Spurs were slain 3-1 at St James Park. Nearly twenty years later, a similar result occurred in a League Cup semi-final. The experienced Pat Jennings, the Spurs goalkeeper, looked on astonished by the intense atmosphere in the ground as Brian was sent surging down the Gallowgate End by his brother Dave. Fast-forward nearly thirty years, and it was again 3-1 against Spurs. Brian, Marion, Ian, and all the rest sang *3-1 To The Goldfish Bowl* as a dejected Jermaine Jenas left the field. They were mocking a man who had left the club, accusing life in town as "like living in a goldfish bowl."

Jenas missed the point. That is precisely part of the package in playing for NUFC. The players belong to the fans, they are part of the fans' daily life, and many, such as Supermac and Shearer, and even Ginola, accepted that. If you cannot stand the heat in the Black & White kitchen, then it is time to get out.

Like most of the Black & White tribe, the young Brian was not given a choice about which team he could support. His Dad liked Newcastle, and Fred next door did too, so that was that. Fred's later claim to fame was to set off a major row amongst Mags and Mackems. There was nothing new about that in the region, except it took place in a sheltered housing home, and most of the participants were aged over eighty, including Fred. Some never spoke to each other for weeks after. Other characters in the life of Brian naturally had no choice either. This religion has no article which allows teenagers to choose a club when they are ready.

Elderly fans clash in NUFC-SAFC derby

There was no choice for Scotty, who angrily refused to look at the Sunderland's 1973 FA Cup when Dennis Tueart brought it back to his Walker home, offering young kids a chance to touch it. He still insists that Tueart was born in Wallsend and not Walker, ignoring the fact that the footballer was brought up in the latter area. The same Scotty became a close mate of Brian when they worked in residential care. Scotty claimed that he was never too involved in cup runs, as he was a league man. This was a curious statement, given that Newcastle last won the league in 1927.

No choice for Steve, who became Father Steve. Fr Steve did hospice work before being seconded to a his parish at Lobley Hill in Gateshead. On moving there, Fr Steve introduced himself to an increasingly intrigued flock by announcing he had to bury a malicious rumour circulating about him. He told his listeners that the previous priest had been wrong to tell people that he, Fr Steve, was a Sunderland fan, and that he wanted to squash that story immediately. He was serious.

No choice either for Brian's older brother Dave, whose caution when predicting United results owed much to his forecast in 1980 that the Wolves centre forward Steve Bull was useless, only for Dave and the group see the striker bang in four goals. At one point brother Dave, exiled to the South of England, ended up driving a disabled Sunderland fan to away games, and was forced to sit at the front of a few thousand Mackems every other week. He also drove the same fan and his wife to Spain. Dave visited the museum of a local Spanish club sporting his Black & White top, and they were relegated a year later.

Definitely no choice for Brian's daughter Claire. Fresh into primary school, Claire asked her Dad if she could go into the pub playground as a bunch of Cornish and Timbuktoo Man U fans mocked as their fourth goal crashed into the net in the 1996 Charity Shield match. Then there was Nellie, aged 88, who appeared in a sheltered housing national magazine wearing her full Black & White strip, complete with shorts and socks; Terry, who featured in the Evening Chronicle on more than one occasion, showing off the most NUFC decorated house in town, from toilet to table, and from bedroom to bathroom; Ian too, who entered a UEFA competition to buy tickets for the final in 2007. The tickets arrived two days after United crashed out against Alkmaar in familiar, humiliating style.

No choice either for Carla, Piper, Geordie; or for another character, who years later sobered up immediately in a car destined for Merseyside when the driver mentioned that he had forgotten to empty the boot with the guns in. He was a poacher back in Chopwell. Another character deserves mention, Kev. He imposed United on his daughters, and his eldest Jessica has never actually seen Newcastle win. She had lived abroad, but has made it to St. James and various other locations.

No choice then for the Mags, for the ones in this book and for all those Mags not in it. Even David, who arrived in Durham City as a youngster and was asked who he supported. He opted for Black & White. His mother Marion then no choice but to take him to games over the years, even after they moved back South. This led Marion to make marathon car journeys from Essex to Newcastle and on to European cities. On one such occasion Marion found herself facing the guns of the Belgrade police who were looking extremely anxious to use them on the Newcastle fans – this against the background of Serbian relations with the West.

More recently, Marion cruelly enticed little Emily, aged six, and living in Kent, to her first game at Fulham away. They witnessed a poor display, lifted only by an Obafemi Martens goal. Emily was hooked, and thought it was magic. She will learn and has a life ahead of her with some wonderful highs and perhaps more numerous lows ahead of her. She also has to spend her childhood alone amongst supporters of various other clubs, which will no doubt include a hefty collection of Man United followers.

This same lack of choice no doubt applies to the well-documented list of famous Mags, including Cardinal Basil Hume. He and Fr Steve would discuss business, only for the meeting to focus mainly on the fortunes of United. The Cardinal once appeared on a local newspaper billboard, with the headline stating "United Fan Could Be Next Pope." Cardinal Hume never made it to the Vatican, but later asked his boss if he could retire, in order to concentrate upon contemplation, fishing, and not least, watching his football team. The Pope refused, which might just prove that Popes are infallible after all.

There's Tim Healy, and Brendan Foster. When one football pundit suggested that Newcastle fans had to be more patient. Brendan seemed to go red with anger, suggesting that half a century without domestic trophies was not a natural recipe for patience. There's Ant and Dec, who would be brilliant comperes for a Mags' "Big Brother" household if ever one was created; Steve Harmison, born in Ashington, who has to check on his team's progress when he plays cricket for England. The list is endless, and includes Brian Johnson, originally of the pop group Geordie, and who moved on to greater fame with AC/DC; the actor Robson Green, and so it goes on. Sting is best left unmentioned, along with Tony Blair, as many suspect that both never really belonged to the Tribe.

Gender is no barrier to NUFC membership, as the likes of Denise Welch, Michelle Heaton, Donna Air, Honor Blackman and so many others confirms. Gabby Logan is a kind of exception on the lack of choice issue, but once she arrived in the region, she fell straight into the Black & White web.

One special figure who does belong to the tribe is of course Alan Shearer himself, who spent his time as a lad dreaming of wearing the famous Number 9 shirt. The lack of choice still applies, as any glance at a baby in a pushchair, dressed in a tiny Black & White strip, confirms. The tradition is alive and kicking, and quite often brings with it a very big kick in the teeth.

These more famous names have no ranking in the Toon Army, which acquired that name in the 1990s after being tagged the Mags in previous decades. They are part of the Black & White Freemasonry, a bond which links fans almost in a family way. This bond leads them all to walk up to the ground built just next to the old public hanging site, which has of course been blamed for the curse which many believe determines the fate of this club.

Chapter Three

Early baptisms at St James Park

Most remember something of their first home game at Gallowgate, named for the obvious reason previously mentioned. Many experienced boredom, disappointment, or even despair; but having tasted the drug, they want more. Some enjoy a win, a triumph, or utter joy. Brian's Claire, in her Rite of Passage, was one of the lucky ones, but as is often the case in one quite young, cannot remember the details. Claire only recalls being unfazed by the noise around her. Aged six, she was lifted up in the air four times as Aston Villa went down 4-3. The blokes, and the woman from Chester-le-Street, insisted that she should come to every match if this was going to happen.

On the other hand, her Dad was one of the unlucky ones. Also aged six, he first tasted life in the Leazes End. More importantly, it was the bloody FA Cup. Newcastle's opponents were non-league Bedford Town. In retrospect, Brian sensed that this was no ordinary game. It was THAT BLOODY FA CUP. His main memory, apart from bewilderment and excitement at being in the stadium and listening to the noise, was of despair.

He could not remember who took him, although it might have been his Dad, but he does remember the dark mood as United crashed out. Brian did not realise he had just joined a famous tradition. Not of winning the FA Cup – that was before he was born in 1957 – but of plunging out against lowly opposition or, alternatively, of the team just not turning up when it really, really mattered.

Years later, Ian, by then a leading Gateshead councillor and dedicated ticket organiser for a large number of Mags, was due to make a speech in Bedford. He checked with Brian to confirm that Newcastle had once played against them. An irritated Brian said they had, and that phone call stirred vague but unhappy memories.

Brian's Black & White life course was set that day at the age of six. Within months, he was tasting the other, glorious side of life as a Mag. He was also more aware of what was actually going on. It was a top-of-the-table clash, albeit in Division 2 against Northampton Town. This was a 5-1 triumph, and whilst Northampton do not rank as a Barcelona or Madrid on the world stage, it was a triumph nevertheless. It sent the crowd into raptures.

The return to the top league was on its way. The buzz was electric, and he wanted more. Anybody recognise that sentiment?

Chapter Four

Football, football everywhere

Throughout these early days of childhood, football was a big part of his life. Brian lived in a very troubled and traumatic house. His Dad worked hard on the local coal trucks, repairing them with pride and skill, helping the exit of the black gold from the region to distant parts. The region of course got little back in return from London governments. Brian's Dad continued to grapple with his own internal pains and anger, attempting to resolve them by a combination of drinking and gambling on donkeys, technically known as horses. He also did "Spot the Ball" and the Pools. Many years later, he actually had a win on the Pools, just missing out on a fortune. A certain team, who had not won away for months, scored in the last minute at West Ham to ruin his chances of a far bigger win: no prizes for guessing the name of that team.

On the serious side, those early days at home were a time of anxiety and distress. The drunken side of the old man's personality was a nasty, and potentially violent one. In that state he provoked much fear, outside and inside the house, but never actually hit his sons. Brian escaped, forgot, dismissed it all, by kicking a football around for hours on end, and developing his Mag credentials and contacts.

At the local Catholic primary school,

Last-minute United winner robs
Dad of big pools win

Brian soon became a major player. He had a key
midfield role at such exotic locations as Dubmire,
Hetton le Hole, and not least Bog Row, which - as
they say in football - was always a difficult place
to go to. The local derby against the Protestant
school was the only occasion when tension
between the two religious communities existed,
although it had nothing to do with religion. Many
of them lived on the same estate as Brian,
although some of them, including Norman, were
Sunderland fans.

Far more important was the fact that
Brian was growing up with other Mags. There
were older ones like Nobby – not Solano – and
Tosser. Brother Dave had his own set of United
contacts, including Micky, Big Ronnie, and not
least Kevin and Peter, the sons of Molly McGee.

Kev and Peter later took brother Dave to occasional away games in their car before he reached his teens. Kevin re-emerged decades later as a Dean taxi-driver in Gateshead. He met Dave's younger sibling, spoke about the olden days for a couple of minutes, and then spent the rest of the journey talking about Newcastle United.

Brian meanwhile had discovered Frankie, Davie, and above all, Steve, as in the future Fr Steve. These two became soulmates, united in United. Steve's family had a fine Black & White tradition. His own father, Joe, his uncle Pat, and as time passed, his younger brothers, Paul, Mick, and David, were all Mags fans. Years later, Mick would join Brian at away matches and regularly visit the local Catholic Club to bait the SAFC. Mick was to be the one who managed to drop the smuggled bottle of wine onto the ground at Cambridge United.

In those earlier days, the same pastimes were followed all across the region: playing football next to the railway lines against a noisy background of steam tankies and coal wagons; football in the Recreation Park, accurately known as "The Wrek"; football in backyards and on the streets; even causing tension on main road itself. As they all lived on a very big bank, and games was often held up if the ball went down went down to the bottom of the hill. Nobody could be bothered to get it of course.

The same arguments broke out when they played "Gates", which involved trying to score with a tennis ball, usually in the dark. The ball was yellow, so at least they could see it. There was also major tension by the greenhouse belonging to the miserable bloke. He just didn't appreciate the thirty-a-side soccer match near his garden, although the local glazier did. Mass games were arranged on the Redhills, although players could not be picked on grounds of team allegiance, given that the Mags were outnumbered. Brian and Steve organised their own little league, in which Newcastle always seemed to do well. Brian also ran his own marbles and Subbuteo league, and again, surprisingly, the same thing happened.

Brian's holidays usually took him to the glamorous resort of Consett. It was near heaven for him, and not because he was based in a Catholic presbytery where his Aunty Mary was the local housekeeper. It was Near Heaven rather because the priests there had a massive backyard, at least four times as big as the ones on the council estate back home. This allowed space for exciting matches, and yet some more tremendous Newcastle victories as they climbed young Brian's self-created league table. His holiday bag usually consisted of clothes, a Black & White scarf and a football. Football seemed to reach everywhere, even into the confessional box. On one Saturday night, Brian sat trying to think up some sins, only to notice that one of the priests was reading the Football Pink, obviously a wise choice in terms of interest in comparison to listening to some made-up sins.

Back at St James, the occasional treats had continued and carried on into Division 1. Then, on 29th October 1966, came a home derby against Sunderland. United, against a background of fans' unrest against the Board – a very familiar tradition over the years - had signed a new centre forward, Wyn Davies. The Mighty Wyn would later take a very high place in the rankings of all those who have worn that famous No. 9 shirt. Things could now only get better. They didn't. In fact, it all went totally pear-shaped. Wyn could do little as the arch-rivals won 3-0, whilst the young Brian sat on the barrier in the Leazes and fell off – several times.

This dire result was Brian's first experience of real NUFC betrayal, and his first vow that he was "never gannin' back". This phrase was to be repeated over the years by Gus, Fr Steve, Geordie, and so many others. As a vow, this phrase was actually meaningless, as they and so many others ALWAYS came back, even Fr Steve who normally kept his vows. On that day – and there were worse days – Brian had to return to a SAFC-majority village. How could they? How could his beloved United have done this to me? he thought.

After that calamitous derby, Brian was lost and vulnerable, but worse was to come. A part of his life was about to take place which he prefers to forget. It's a very dark secret indeed, but one to which he has to admit. Brian's excuse for remaining silent all these years is a valid one, given his age and state of mind at the time. Brian's eldest brother Michael was the Red & White sheep inside the family. Michael kidnapped his younger sibling, and started to take him to Roker Park for a few games. On arrival at the ground, Michael would push Brian through a turnstile and go off to the pub, returning to meet him at the front of the Paddock. Brian was uncomfortable, and fortunately, this painful episode in his life did not last long.

Not for nothing was Brian named after Brian, the ancient Irish King who drove out the Danes and anybody else from the Emerald Isle. Our Brian rebelled, fought back, and within a very short spell was back at Gallowgate for good, or bad, scarred but having survived his enforced presence at Roker Park

The mid-to-late 1960s were marked by various memories for young Mags growing up with the club they worshipped. These were the days of "Shoot" on local TV. Incredibly, years later, Mad Mick – co-owner of the Back Page bookshop, fanzine writer, and former football team-mate of Brian when the latter's residential care home workplace put a team in the Walker Lightfoot league, told Brian that many of the "Shoot" archives were destroyed by Tyne Tees. He rightly reckoned that if the programmes were shown again, there would be a guaranteed audience. Certainly, they plugged into the tv in their thousands in those early days.

At 1.55pm every Sunday, the viewing figures for "Farming Outlook" rocketed, although this did not reflect a sudden interest in Northumberland sheep farming. It meant that "Shoot" was due on, and there was a chance to watch the highlights of a North East match, and more than often, a Newcastle match. The streets were emptied of kids for an hour on those Sundays. Commentator George Taylor's voice still echoes for some, although his later replacement, Kenneth Wolstenholme does not. Just because he had commentated upon an England World Cup

win, he seemed disinterested in North East
football. The latter is far more important for most
Mags.

"Shoot" was the big event on screen for
north east football fans at that time. There were
no radio commentaries, which in some ways was
perhaps no bad thing in terms of blood pressure
and anxiety attacks. Nowadays, some listen
intently, pacing the kitchen or bedroom, wisely
undisturbed by children or any other inhabitants,
swearing, shouting, and leaping around in
deranged manners. Frustration does occur when
the actual location of the ball is unknown, or
when the commentators remark that there is no
way he can see United losing this one now. That
invariably leads to the other team going straight
up the pitch and putting a winner into the net.
Some fans refuse to listen, perhaps for health
reasons, including Ian when he is not actually
away at a game.

Kids banned during match commentary

Back in the 60's, "Shoot" had no major rival, unless the BBC's "Match of the Day" is included. But national media coverage of NUFC was not renowned for showing major details of United games. Sky was not even a twinkle in the eye of Rupert Murdoch, and the clandestine matches beamed in from Arabia or South East Asia were not around. Pubs illegally showing football, with curtains drawn, did not exist. Neither did those odd games in one era when the TV picture was a couple of seconds behind a radio commentary, thus causing confusion and anger at anyone who had a radio on at the time.

The mid-to-late 60s, at the crumbling and archaic St James, were the days of the Peanut Man and so many other memories. The Peanut Man, shouting "tanner a bag", was a kind of modern Evening Chronicle salesman in manner and voice style. He had the ability to hit his customers like a professional darts player hitting the bullseye. Brian's cousin Paul flirted with NUFC and came along to one match, spending the whole game waiting for the Peanut Man to come back. Brian was disgusted, and as far as he understands, Cousin Paul never came back. Bigger fool him, Brian thinks, some of the time anyway.

Fans used to climb onto the floodlights in a bigger attendance, and when it snowed, the kids used to sit on the straw at the front – naturally having been passed over the heads of adults down to the front of the packed Leazes. There was a Magpie Mascot, an old bloke dressed in Black & White suit and big hat, who walked around the ground waving, just waving. Those bloody rattles were around too, although Brian

has to admit that he managed to obtain one. Their
noise was worse than that of Ian's whistling in
later years. And there was also the appearance
before kick-off of a brass band playing music,
usually of a military nature. In many ways, those
bands were better than what was to come.

In a different era, supporters have had to
listen to Alan Robson on the Tannoy asking them
to "make some noise for the Lads." Or worse, the
emergence of that bloke on the system at the end
of a match thanking fans for coming and inviting
them to Shearer's bar for a drink. Thanking NUFC
for coming, quite often ill-timed, was absurd. It
was not a local kid's birthday party, for God's
Sake, and Brian, Marion, Gus, and all the others
used to try and shut their ears to such stuff. As for
the invite to the bar named after Big Al, the
announcer made it sound as if free drinks were
available. Marion still laughs at one of the choices
of songs in that later era, when they played *The
Boys Are Back in Town* – this after a very young
United side under Glen Roeder's management
had been hammered.

In the late 60s Brian was taking in some
exciting home games. One stands out in August,
the day after his birthday. It was Happy Birthday
time, which would not always be the case every
August in the future with NUFC, when his
celebrations would be sometimes marred by
events at the club. Brother Dave and his older
group took him to witness a glorious 5-1 home
victory against Chelsea. The Mighty Wyn got two.
Just after Christmas in the same year, a 3-3 draw
at Sunderland saw Ollie Burton scoring two
penalties, and man-mountain John McNamee

swinging on their net in celebration of his goal. Frustratingly, Brian was not allowed to go, something about the potential danger, which of course did not concern him. He would be there soon though, and realise what older Mags were talking about. Those older fans returned to the village content and boastful, and the traditional arguments took place for a few weeks after about just who deserved to win.

In May 1968, Brian saw the title clinched. Not by United of course, but by Manchester City, in a 4-3 defeat. He was now already old enough to resent the success of other clubs, a sign of growing maturity, and a sentiment held by most Mags to this day. Later in life, he checked that game out, and found out that it stopped Manchester United winning the league, so in retrospect it was not such a bad day after all.

Just after Christmas 1969, a packed Leazes took on the Mighty Leeds, and the Mighty Wyn and Pop Robson scored to defeat them 2-1. There was also a glorious battle between Jack Charlton and NUFC centre-half cult hero John McNamee, whenever their paths crossed for a corner. Jack was talented but tough, hard as nails. Mac was less talented but harder than nails. Fans loved him, and always forgave him for his occasional shots which usually ended up on top of the Leazes roof. The atmosphere that day, and throughout this period, was electric, and would get even better in the early 1970s. *Sha La La La MacNamee, Who The Fucking Hell Is He, The Best Centre Half In The Countree, Write Him Down In Historee.*

Queues snaked around the entrances to

get in the Leazes, and the years were passed watching the likes of Jim Iley, *My My My, Jim Iley*, Jim Scott on the wing, Dave Hilley and Trevor Hockey, and Gordon Marshall. Some of the above may have left, but they were all heroes. A certain Frank Clark was around of course. Wyn's songs are well documented, but the Christmas version was a favourite for many: *Oh Come Let Us Adore Wyn, Oh Come Let us Adore Him.*

Years later, Shearer went one better, when Hexham Abbey choir made a special version of a Christmas song in his name.

Chapter Five

School in Sunderland

1968-69 saw two life-changing events in the Black & White Life of Brian, one of far less importance than the other. The less vital one involved news arriving on his Mam's doormat, confirming that he had passed his 11-plus exam. This was part of the ridiculous and unfair system which meant that brother Dave had gone to a sink school, Fr Steve to less of a sink school, and Brian to a so-called school for bright kids, one of the large all-boy Catholic Grammars. The girls were down the road, unfortunately.

This new place for his future studies was bitterly sectarian. Most will know, and will be proud of the fact, that this region has little time for the religious divides common in the West of Scotland and the North of Ireland. All know that there is a sectarian divide of a different kind, namely relations between Newcastle and Sunderland supporters. A drunken Glaswegian once asked Brian, Sam, and Lofty in an Edinburgh nightclub which team was the Protestant one. They laughed and added that was all their local rivalry needed, a religious split as well.

The problem in the new school was that it attracted lads from Seaham to South Shields, from parts of Felling, Chester-le-Street, and other parts of the North East. This was a recipe for disaster. Worse, the place itself was located in

Sunderland, but once again, Brian was far from isolated, given the geographical intake of its pupils.

Having recovered from the fact that he was off to school in the capital of the Mackems, Brian met other Mags, including Kev from South Shields, who was extremely bright and devoted to NUFC. Others included characters from Chester and Boldon, as well as the Felling twins. A younger Mag later emerged, Kevin from Felling. Kevin would play in midfield alongside Brian, and later still, unfortunately, play for Sunderland until he went off to Arsenal. The older Mags were already there, and included Micky, one of brother Dave's mates, and Big Ned, who came in useful when attempts were made to set younger kids' hair on fire on the bus.

The Mag link ensured Brian was normally protected by Micky and Big Ned. Black & White United scarves were worn on the way to school and back, and Brian proudly carried a Black & White painted haversack with NUFC on the back of it. This did have some risk before reaching the bus station to get out of town, as other schools were all full of SAFC.

Inevitably, Sunderland fans emerged in Brian's new life. One or two became good mates, including Jess and SAFC Kev. Jim was in his class, and he later became a Red & White fanzine founder. Crossing paths in the 90s, he confirmed from his office in Longbenton that he hated Newcastle more than ever, which quite impressed his former Mag schoolmate at the other end of a phone call related to work.

A truce reigned against this background

of a divided school, save for the occasional compass fight or attempted bullying incident. As stated, the Mags had a presence, although they were outnumbered. The truce had to operate, or anarchy would have taken over. Arguments were generally limited to preoccupations such as ripping out maps of the North East and debating which area had the most NUFC or SAFC. With the inevitable exception of Newcastle and Sunderland, other towns were simply up for grabs, and SAFC Kev would claim Boldon and Chester-le-Street, and Brian would hotly dispute such nonsense. SAFC Kev even tried to claim Gateshead and South East Northumberland at one point.

Groups would gather around to choose the North East national team to play against England, but it was never long before that discussion broke down. As these school years passed, SAFC Kev and Brian would swop stories on away matches, and formed a kind of common bond when discussing visits to some of the more notorious venues. They would study, or pretend to study, at St Aidan's until 1975, when South Shields Kev, SAFC Kev, Jess, and Brian all departed for cities further south.

There was a bigger journey on the horizon, which proved to be far more important. It was to Budapest. The biggest Black & White event in the Life of Brian, and of so many others, was just around the corner. The Fairs Cup is a major trophy, although not an English one. As it turned out, it's been the only one to date in Brian's life, unless people really want to include the Texaco Cup, the Anglo-Italian Cup, the obscure Japan Cup, the mysterious Inter-Toto Cup, and possibly even the Chopwell Memorial Cup or whatever.

It all began in a rather curious fashion. United qualified for Europe on the inter-city rule, which allowed only one team from one city to enter the Fairs Cup. A rare event had occurred when Manchester United actually did Newcastle a favour. The Mancs won the European Cup the year before, thus automatically qualifying for that competition, and opening up an extra place in the Fairs Cup. Some of the teams above the Magpies, who finished tenth, could not enter - their own fault for having two clubs in one city. Anyway, the rule might as well have said a team with a name beginning with an *N and an E and a WC*, and ending in a *TLE*, could have qualified. It did not matter to the fans. European nights beckoned.

And what nights they were! Heaven to be with NUFC, and with the bus which took off from the youth club back in the village. Big Ronnie, brother Dave, Fr Steve, Joe, the local teacher Colin, and Tarmac Nobby. They all lived and breathed United. Nobby was a fierce-looking character, but with a heart of gold – well, for fellow Mags that is. Over the years, he passed many a happy hour baiting the local Red & Whites, and once stunned passers-by in a local pub by asking them to leave. They happened to have dropped into a bar on their way back to Pennywell, and the two skinheads were mocking Newcastle. This was a fatal mistake, given that they didn't know who was in the place, not least Nobby. All that was in the future.

That packed Fairs Cup bus left the village

in search of glory in that previous era. They all crammed into a floodlit St James to see the Mighty Wyn unleash his aerial terror and bombardment. They stood, or rather swayed in the old Popular side, watching little Pop Robson, the little Danish genius Benny Arentoft, Willie McFaul, and all the others take United to the quarters against Victoria Setubal in a North-East snowstorm.

Off to Fairs Cup triumph

Then came Glasgow Rangers in the semi-final and three pitch invasions, two from the Jocks in anger and one from the Leazes in celebration. Bottles and cans rained down on the Popular. Some were returned back to the Rangers fans, as they reacted rather badly to their defeat. Brian and Fr Steve managed to get lost in town after the match, narrowly avoiding crowds of angry

Orangemen. Brian remains grateful to this day
that those Orangemen could not see into the
future and thus have known the future career of
one of his best mates.

The final itself was one of those times –
and there are times – when it was heaven to be a
Mag. Brian was hurled around a delirious Leazes
End as United beat Ujpest Doza 3-0, with Bobby
Moncur getting two of them. Then off to Budapest
with Moncur scoring again in a 3-2 victory. Bobby
never scored much but certainly picked his
moments. *They Call Us Newcastle United, They
Call Us The Team Of The Land, And Here's To
Bobby Moncur, With The Fairs Cup In His Hand*.
The bigger half of the North East football
fraternity somersaulted into chaos, and joy and
euphoria reigned supreme. The Felling twins,
whose family must have had some money – away
travel to Europe was not within the grasp of many
– brought a programme back from Budapest for
Brian. He kept it lovingly, despite the fact he
could not understand a word it said, until his
oldest brother Michael managed to have a flood
in his garage, wiping out the entire family
collection. That matters little to Brian. They won
it.

School life in Sunderland was bliss.
Interestingly, many Mags felt United did not get
enough credit from the London-based media for
this incredible triumph. They were right, but they
would all soon become accustomed to this over
the years. With some notable exceptions, United
were often dismissed, even as entertainers. Many
believe that the BBC in London were biased,
ranging from characters such as Jimmy Hill all the

way to Alan Hansen in the present day, although Alan Shearer is trying to rectify that now. The same suspicion has been directed at certain newspapers which seem to revel in some crisis surrounding the club. Admittedly the club and certain players have certainly contributed to some of these crises.

Mags prefer their fanzines, NUFC.com website, and despite some scepticism at times, the local papers. Give them John Gibson, for example, one of the best and most knowledgeable writers on United. None of this mattered. It still does not. If most of that media back in 1969 wanted to predict how majestic Spurs were, how wonderful West Ham were, how creative Chelsea were, that was up to them.

Europe continued, but never on the scale of the Cup victory. One particular match in March 1970, raised just about every emotion that football fans, and particularly NUFC supporters, have experienced. The village group once again swayed in the Popular as United pulled back a 2-0 deficit to go 3-0 up in front of 60,000 people. They felt cautious, nervous, hopeful, and finally euphoric. Well, not finally.

With minutes to go, Anderlecht, their Belgian opponents, scored and went through on the away goals rule. Who the hell introduced that? It's nearly as bad as the penalty shoot-out rule. The mood turned to utter and complete despair for the near-60,000 crowd, and the many thousands not in the ground.

Chapter Six

Getting Away

Brian's educational development with the club was advancing apace, with home League games and European nights. Another bridge had to be crossed, the other Rite of Passage: away matches. In March 1970, just turning into his teens, he took off for his first away game. It was a Good Friday. And it was not a long journey by the standards of Newcastle travels. It was at Sunderland. Good Friday is misappropriately named for many reasons, not least in Christian religious terms. And in football, this game was certainly not a Good Friday by any standards. The departure from the family home itself caused some bother, as Brian's Mam seemed annoyed that he and brother Dave, were not going to the Stations of the Cross, and were gannin' to the match, as the phrase goes.

Mam should have been far more disturbed about where they were actually going, as they were about to attend one of the most violent North East derbies in recent times, which made battles in Bath Lane and at Seaburn look like a Vicar's tea-party. Despite myths surrounding the emergence of football hooliganism, there had been a history between these two clubs. In 1901, a riot had broken out, yes, on a Good Friday, and the game never started. In 1909 the players were unable to get to the tunnel at half-time due to the fighting. But in modern times, this particular exchange was pretty grim.

The song says it all; *We Took The Fulwell, We Took The Shed, The Leazes End Boot Boys Left The Bastards Dead*. Fortunately, not dead, but for a considerable time, the Fulwell End of the SAFC was occupied by thousands of Mags, with the police trying to oust the visitors, and the Sunderland fans trying even harder to eject them. The latter were partially helped by a sack of weapons thrown over into the end by Mags which landed into the arms of the hosts. It was total chaos, inside and outside the ground, and the journey back was a bit fraught for Shiney-based Black & Whites as they had to pass through the town itself to catch their bus. There was no over-the-top police operation in those days. They managed to pull their scarves out of their jeans as they left the Pennywell area, which marked the official border with Sunderland.

This in itself led to some further incidents on a mixed bus which was heading back to the village and beyond up to Consett. Inevitably, over the following months, local characters told of, and exaggerated, their roles in the events of Good Friday. Big Sid, a Red & White, claimed he led the charge against the Mags, but it was later discovered he was not even at the match. One of the local NUFC boasted that he fought on the Wearmouth Bridge, but his statement did not fit with the fact that he left Seaburn for home in a car.

After this, most early away matches were tame in comparison. Brian ventured out of the region as the away bug took root, and soon a very major player entered his life: Geordie, raised in

the village and of good United stock, via his father
Tom. His Dad had installed a love of NUFC in his
son and his friendship with Brian was inevitable,
given that they lived on the same estate. Geordie
was apparently bullied for a short while as a
youngster, which ensured that he had developed
a very tough streak. He was never bullied again.
He was desperate to get to away games, and as Fr
Steve was a home-only fan in this era, a new
partnership was formed for travel purposes.

At first brother Dave played the key role
in away games, taking Brian to Nottingham and
Huddersfield in 1971. That visit to West Yorkshire
was bleak, at a ground set against the backdrop
of rain-sodden Pennines, with a Kop called the
Cow Shed and some Mags inside it. The game was
boring, but the away bug was now well inside the
system. Geordie and Brian soon took off further
afield, very much kindred spirits, Mags and
intensely proud of it. By the end of the year, they
had their first meeting with Piper, at West Brom,
who, to this day, is a well-known fanatic and
NUFC traveller, with a match-day base in the Irish
Centre shared by some of Brian's mates and
contacts.

Piper is a Stalwart, and is affectionately
known by many amongst the Geordie tribe and
beyond. Brian bumped into him in the Haymarket
in the late 90s, on their way to the Irish Club, and
the walk took far longer than usual. He felt he
was in the company of a superstar – he was – and
Piper was constantly stopped by United fans on
the street and outside bars. One Saturday night a
rumour once rocked Felling, his home town, that
he had died. The pubs, including the Fox, were

bombarded by telephone calls from around the country, from Cockneys and Scousers, and so on asking if it was true. Much alarm was created, until he surfaced in the Holly Hill Club the night after the away match.

It was good to meet Piper, and some other fellow travellers that wintry day. Back at West Brom in December 1971, Geordie, Piper, and Brian, along with quite a few others, joyfully embraced the song, *Jingle Bells, Jingle Bells, Jingle All The Way, Oh What Fun It Is To See United Win Away,* as Viv Busby and Supermac did the damage in a 3-0 win. By 1972, the youngsters were visiting further afield, and one occasion was particularly memorable. Not because of a 2-1 defeat at Crystal Palace, but due to the fact that the pair found themselves on the same train back as the team itself. In later decades, when footballers would be treated with far more luxury, such a plot could not have occurred, but, with the players sitting in the first class, the pair ventured nervously up. The great Terry Hibbitt was standing at an entrance into their carriage, and just told the lads to wait a minute. He returned with autographs, and the real prize captured: the signature of a certain Malcolm MacDonald, Supermac, the latest hero in town.

This feat would only be surpassed many years later when brother Dave, spotting Alan Shearer filming on the Quayside, picked up a beer mat and asked if the Lion of Gosforth would sign it for his niece, Claire. He did, and it remains on her bedroom table, not to be moved. Geordie and Brian rounded off their year with a Boxing Day visit to Leeds – it was always Boxing Day there anyway, even if the match took place in the late autumn.

During these years, Geordie and Brian, and others, were now visiting such exotic locations as Leicester, Derby and Stoke, as well as continuing with trips to the less exotic London. Their early ventures had been confined to travel with the official Supporters' Clubs buses which left from Morden Street in the town. They met other Mags of course, but soon began to resent the element of discipline imposed upon the travellers, such as being told to hide colours and avoid gesticulating at rival fans. As their time with this kind of away travel drew to an end, there was one occasion when they regretted missing the official bus. It was partly because they looked as if they would not make it to Wolverhampton, and mainly because rescue came in the shape of a van pulling up with two far more senior Mags on board.

At first, the offer seemed fantastic, but as the vehicle began to tour the East End, Longbenton, Benton, Denton, Kenton, and moved onto the West End, knocking dodgy characters out of bed and picking up equally dodgy characters on street corners, it became obvious that the youngsters were now in a van packed with NUFC hard-core hooligans - big time. They were friendly enough to the two kids, apart from seizing their pack of sandwiches and eating them all in an instant, although one of them did say thanks. Well out of their league, Geordie and Brian were alarmed when a serious row broke out as they reached the M6. An Arsenal bus was spotted going in the opposite direction to Carlisle, and some of the characters wanted the driver to turn around and catch it up. Including the two kids, the numbers count reached twelve. It was pointed out that there were about fifty Cockneys on the said bus. Fortunately, the driver insisted that they had to carry on South, adding that time was vital if the van were serious about taking the North Bank at Wolves.

Arriving in that welcoming West Midlands town, parking up near the ground itself, they discussed tactics and added that Geordie and Brian could come with them. Cowardice, or wisdom, took over, and the pair slunk off quietly. Sure enough, ten minutes into the game, the Wolves kop erupted. Several characters were finally ejected by the police, and taken up to the United end to a warm applause and hero's welcome.

Like the 1980s, this was an era of football hooliganism, simply a fact of life. Fans had to learn how to be street-wise, and fight if they had to, even if they were not hard-core. Nobody thought anything of travelling back from a match with the bus windows out, only noticing that it sometimes got cold when the A1 was reached. In fact, the broken windows allowed supporters, including Brian and Geordie, to wave scarves in sight of any other travelling opposition groups. By now, the two were regularly on unofficial trips, whether by bus or using the train. Sometimes, it was a big relief to see some of the older crews, often led by Doddsy, at some platform, when surrounded by a crowd of Derby or Brummie hooligans for example. Usually, most mobs retreated after assessing the nature of such Mag crews.

Odd incidents took place during that period. A bunch of United fans were taken aback at one would-be attack in Coventry, when a group of skinheads ran towards them. All held their ground, but were baffled when they realised that most of the assailants were female. The Geordies decided to growl, and just look menacing – easy for them to do – and the ladies quickly changed their minds. At Sheffield United, Brian looked curiously at Geordie covering his left eye during the match, and asked why he was doing that. Geordie explained that he was protecting himself from the missiles and bricks, seemingly oblivious to the fact that the rest of his head remained extremely vulnerable. They stayed in the same spot anyway.

Kings Cross in London was never much fun, as the Cockneys seemed to unite in huge numbers to attack any Northern visitors after the matches. Allegiances were made with Sheffield Wednesday or any other fans heading up the line to counter-attack the Cockneys and get on the trains, but it has to be said that Brian never witnessed any temporary alliance with Leeds. Newcastle and Leeds just seemed to battle each other, quite often without a Cockney in sight. This was the 1970s, but none of it stopped the enjoyment, the buzz, of being away representing the Mag nation.

Chapter Seven

I was born in the Leazes End

Back at St James, the two young Mags had firmly
settled in their second, or perhaps first home: *The
Leazes End, Where Geordies Never End, And All
The Chelsea Fans Lie Dead At Our Feet*. A myth
later emerged that the Gallowgate was always the
true home for United fans. There is some truth in
that assertion, but in this era, the Leazes
dominated, and those fans saw some pretty
attractive performances, and helped the team do
it. What could be an exciting team never set the
league alight, but Joe Harvey was putting together
a side with flair, able to beat anybody on their
day, particularly at St. James.

One such occasion was the victory
against the very mighty Liverpool in August 1971.
It should be added that the triumph was assisted
by an equally mighty Malcolm MacDonald home
debut, complete with hat-trick, as he was carried
off soon afterwards to sounds of *Supermac,
Superstar, How Many Goals Have You Scored So
Far?*

One home game in the Cup is best left
unmentioned, in front of 40,000 fans, when non-
league Hereford earned a 2-2 draw. The away
replay is simply erased from the memory of many,
or rather would be, if it was not for the BBC
showing the Hereford goal every year when FA
Cup time comes around. Hereford of course

caused intense pain and anger, and when Newcastle visited Old Trafford days later, and won there on a very rare occasion, this provoked more pain and anger for Brian and many other Mags. Typical, they thought. On a happier note, these were the days of Supermac and John Tudor, a powerful pairing, and a midfield with Jimmy "Jinky" Smith inside it, and Tony Green, only for the latter to suffer a brief, tragic end to his career.

It was later noted that Tony was embarrassed that he only played 30-odd games for the club after they had paid so much money for him. There was no need, Tony. There have been a few NUFC players who should have had that emotion, but he certainly should not have. He is still remembered with affection to this day amongst the older generation. Tony Green aside, there was some dispute in that period over whether "Jinky" or Tommy Cassidy should have been the first name down for the midfield place, and if it came to a crunch, it did lead to fierce arguments amongst some fans, not least Geordie, Brian, Fr Steve, and brother Dave. He opted for the less exciting, but more reliable Cassidy.

All this was roared on by that loud, raucous, fanatical, and sometimes hostile Leazes End. These were glorious days, if not always on the pitch. In more dull moments, on occasions, violent clashes sometimes broke out between the fans. This was the era of the Aggro Boys, and Scotswood Road, Longbenton, Benton, Walker, Denton Burn, would sometimes announce their presence. There was also a rare and usually meek offer from the Washington Aggro Boys. All hell would break loose at whichever area was laying

claim to own the terrace. Skinheads tackled
Hairies, and all this to the bemusement of some
instantly forgettable small away following
elsewhere in the ground who simply did not
understand why the Geordies were fighting each
other. Looking back, neither did Geordie and
Brian, but that was a fact of life then.

Less hostile chants would break out over
Celtic and Rangers, but far more vicious taunts
would invite the police to enter the Leazes in
numbers, and not for a cup of tea either. Songs
like *Harry Roberts Is Our Friend, He Kills Coppers,*
and *We All Agree, Liddle Towers Was Murdered,*
would echo around the ears of the lined-up pigs,
as they were affectionately known. Perhaps the
most amusing tale of all was the one when Joe
Harvey told Bertie Mee that he had not heard of
North Bank, Highbury – but he had heard of the
Leazes Aggro. Joe was many, many things, but
whether he would have boasted about the Leazes
Aggro is doubtful.

There is no doubt that Joe would have
boasted about the noise those fans made when
his side were in search of a lift. When that
Newcastle team needed the Leazes behind them
on the pitch, they got their backing twice over
and more. The famous Bill Shankly once
expressed his own amazement, when they sang
United, United, for twenty minutes against his
Liverpool side. Later in life, Brian would meet
many ex-Leazes Enders, such as Terry with the
famous Black & White house, and Nick, whose
look at Cardiff in 2005 said it all. In this era,
though, Geordie was his companion, and they
sang with pride and passion, members of the Mag

frontline. It has to be said that Geordie did do one strange thing in his time there, when he actually arranged a date and met her near the goal. Hardly a weekend in Paris, and the relationship did not last. Brian equalled this in a different way, by wearing a wedding suit, complete with flower, for one match, but more of that later.

The songs are simply too many to mention. One favourite was *I Was Born in the Leazes End,* to the tune of a Lee Marvin song. Perhaps the best of all was heard in the passion, hope and pride, when they all sang *We Shall Overcome, We Shall Overcome, We Shall Overcome Someday, Oh Deep In Our Hearts, We Do Believe, We Shall Overcome Someday.* The song was more associated with the American civil rights movement and with Northern Ireland, but the Mags meant it. They really did believe that, one day, they would overcome.

Away from life in the NUFC home, Brian's family troubles continued, but his Mam and brothers kept a sense of humour which helped them all get by. One night, his Dad left the house to burn down the local Catholic Church, only to return. He'd forgotten the matches. By this stage, Brian was taking on a major role inside that house, trying to deal with the chaos and bloody trauma. On one occasion he saw his Mam slumped in blood, having drunk a bottle of whisky. Normally, she never drank.

One late and sleepless night nearly led to a serious suspension from school, and possibly worse. Brian was asked by a certain teacher in an aggressive manner what he thought that he was doing arriving at 10.00am in the morning? Given the teacher had nothing to do with him, and Brian was feeling a bit strained, he gave the teacher an Anglo-Saxon response in front of a little gang of more junior pupils and was forced by the Head to apologise. The Head liked Brian, as he played football and tennis for the school, and privately asked him to say sorry, which he did in a very disgruntled manner. A cancer scare with his Mam was also a worrying time.

But life went on, and it went on with NUFC. Away from St James, Geordie and Brian would often pass the night in the former's kitchen, playing darts, and talking about any news coming out of the club. On other occasions, it was time to catch up with the other locals in the quarry or at the tip for a bit crack. But United was their life. Brian had little time for lasses, or to be more accurate, they had little time for him. He blamed this on the fact that he could not grow a beard, as one potential love had run off with an older lad – with a beard. Another girl had finished him when he took off for an away match instead of opting for a day out in Whitley Bay.

One disastrous romance, which lasted about two weeks, is best left unmentioned. She was a Sunderland fan. It would be some years later before women played a major role in Brian's Black & White life, and learned how to live with both him and NUFC.

Some Mags in the village in that era of darts in Geordie's kitchen passed their time away in occupations such as spray-painting United slogans on stations and derelict walls around the area, in Boldon, Chester-le-Street, Shiney, and even, in Sunderland itself. Others took up hobbies such as hanging skeletons in the local graveyard late at night. It was a short-cut from the pub, and apparently used to alarm some of the older villagers after they had had a couple. It may have helped some of them give up alcohol.

Meanwhile, Brian had long since found himself a job. First he was a seller of the Pink – and unfortunately also the Football Echo, its SAFC counterpart. This meant the need for rushed returns from home games and substitutes if he was away. He moved up the ladder to collect the week's paper money, on darker nights accompanied by Geordie as a kind of minder. This freed him from the Saturday night job, and his income rose via his actual pay and the tips, particularly good from the local Mags who knew him from his days selling the Pink. Most of the money was diverted into following United, although as years progressed, some of it ended up in card games in the back room of the Grey Horse, not a place famous for crackdowns on under-age drinking.

A major new United fan was now a key figure in NUFC life in the village - Gordon the FishShopOwner. He was a vital man to know for two main reasons. One was he always gave the local Mags extra helpings in his fish shop, and would reopen the door if Geordie and Brian, or any other Mags, were returning late from somewhere after he had shut up shop. The other reason was particularly significant, as he was soon taking the pair and brother Dave to the match in his car, with a lift back guaranteed. Gordon was a fearsome-looking character, with some kind of plate buried in his forehead as a result of a car accident. His wife Maria was equally fearsome, although it has to be said, far more attractive.

It goes without saying that the local SAFC did not cross this couple, partly as their chip rations would have been further reduced, and mainly because any anti-NUFC comments would have seen them leave the shop, and not through the door either.

Chapter Eight

One wedding & two funerals

The years of 1973 and 1974 were a particularly traumatic period for the followers of Newcastle United Football Club, along with some difficult times for North East miners, although their pain did not last as long. Two FA Cup Finals took place, or rather two funerals in terms of their impact upon the Mags. There was also a major family wedding in the life of Brian, which explains his appearance in the Leazes complete with wedding suit and flower, which he forgot to remove, until reminded by Geordie.

United embraced the FA Cup in 1973, and Gordon and the car load set off for the home tie against Luton in fine mood. He had a seat, with his bairn, for the East Stand, which was partially opened up for the first time for this easy stroll against lower league opposition. Only things did not quite go to plan, and by 4.45pm that Saturday afternoon, Newcastle were out of the Cup. Bad moods would be an understatement on this occasion. Some motorcyclist tried to cut across Gordon's car just next to the Tyne Bridge, and it is perhaps best left unrecorded what happened next. The air was blue, and although he did open the fish shop that night, no football talk was allowed. Meanwhile, back in town, attempts were made to smash Supermac's new boutique, as some fans felt that he had not tried enough, which in retrospect was a bit harsh.

All this could be handled. Something else was on the horizon which simply could not be handled at all. Sunderland began to sneak their way towards the FA Cup Final, and the village witnessed the emergence of Red & White scarves which had not seen daylight for many years. Tension mounted for Brian, Geordie, Tarmac Nobby, brother Dave, Fr Steve and all the rest, as Wembley was reached. For perhaps the only occasion on record, they all turned into Leeds fans, and no longer sang *Leeds, Leeds, And Leeds, And Leeds, Who The Fucking Hell Are Leeds?* All were convinced that this nightmare would be ended by one of the best sides ever seen in modern English football.

Brian's Red & White brother travelled off, and the Black & White Mam opened up the house for guests. Loyal to her oldest son, she, like the rest, wanted Leeds to hammer Sunderland. Ian Porterfield scored that goal, and Montgomery saved against Lorimer. Some bodies were on Mam's floor, as they thought the ball had gone in. Another Monty was of course well-known to some of the older villagers from their days in the desert, fighting Rommel. But this Monty had pulled off an incredible save, perhaps not quite comparable to the victory in World War 2, but to the younger Mags, his name would become far more etched on their minds than that of the British Army leader. And then, at the end, Bob Stokoe, himself a former Geordie Cup hero, ran across Wembley with that bloody trilby on.

Back in the house, for some inexplicable reason, Jackie, a SAFC fan with a broken leg, had managed to get himself into the sitting room, and tried to catch Brian as the latter stormed out of the house in the direction of the river. The rest of the evening saw crowded pubs celebrating the Cup win, Geordie and the others just wandering around aimlessly and in a state of shock. If ever a Jesmond-style Support Group was needed, it was on that awful night. Meanwhile, Gordon, in his fish shop empire, was surrounded by steam totally unrelated to the cod cooking on his burners.

Frying tonight - Gordon the FishShopOwner steams at SAFC Cup win

It took time to recover from this. Newcastle did play in one final, a month later. They beat Florence – the football team, not Andy Capp's wife - in the Anglo-Italian Cup, thus lifting a trophy, well, a sort of trophy. Somehow, it did not rank alongside the FA Cup, although some defiant

Mags at least tried to claim some success in the face of the gloating Red & Whites in the village. Brian had to do the same thing at that school in Sunderland, although his heart was not really in it.

The following season was now a case of, follow that. United never really set the league alight, although some of their football was exciting. One league match in October is worthy of mention. Well, it did involve the wedding of the Red & White brother. Brian's main worry was the match, scheduled for the afternoon, against Chelsea. After some discussion, he was allowed to sit between the newly-weds in the honeymoon car, which took off from Easington and dropped him at the Central Station.

Brian was wearing a hideous seventies-style flaired suit – purple - with flower in lapel, and a Black & White scarf. He raced up to the Leazes, found Geordie and some others near their normal spot. They did not comment that he was late, but rather reminded him that this was not normal attire for the famous terrace. This was long before the days of corporate boxes and the like, and they were right about his choice of clothes. Brian took off the flower, said that would do the trick, and the team did the trick as well, with Supermac putting two past Chelsea. Another memorable wedding, thanks to Malcolm.

This was not a season for the league. This was a season for the Cup. The other Cup, the League Cup, never really took off, and only deserves mention for historical reasons. The fans invaded the pitch against Doncaster Rovers in a 6-1 home victory. Frank Clark had scored. Frank never scored, and the crowd went ballistic. The

Late for game, Brian dashes from wedding

baffled Doncaster players, witnessing such celebrations, must surely have wondered where on earth they were. They were hardly giants of the game, yet those United fans seemed ecstatic. *Frank Clark Knows My Father, Father Knows Frank Clark,* as Terry and Ian still sing in the Irish Centre occasionally to this day.

There was only one Cup that really mattered though, particularly after the events of

1973, and Newcastle had to win it. The run to Wembley got off to a stuttering start, with non-league Hendon taking United back to North London for a replay. The fourth round also saw a stumble, when Scunthorpe managed to do the same thing. Geordie and Brian travelled down there and witnessed a decent victory, propelling the team into the fifth round. It was a strange occasion, as the pair should have been at school. The game took place on a Wednesday afternoon, due to a ban on floodlights.

The miners were having their own cup tie with Ted Heath's Tory Government, in a re-run of a previous match against the Tories in 1972. These were was hard times for the village and the North East pit families. In the 1974 fixture, the miners won, Heath lost.

It was determined that the Fish Shop Must Go On. Geordie, Brian, and a couple of others, spent some time scavenging underneath old coal board trucks on the railway lines, filling up sacks of very poor versions of the black gold, partly to ensure the Fish Shop still functioned. It was the least they could do for Gordon. On one occasion, they had to make a very hasty exit when the police headed down the lines, but fortunately, their running abilities were good on that dark night. Coal for Gordon then, and coal for their houses, as they always took a bag home in the FishShopOwner's car.

That Cup run became a tremor on the Richter scale at West Brom, turning into a full-scale earthquake when Nottingham Forest turned up in the quarters by March. The visit to West Brom was sheer bliss, yet another day when it simply made it all so worthwhile. Jimmy "Jinky" Smith destroyed the Baggies, Supermac did his business, and the rocking away end, packed with bouncing Geordies, celebrated as if they had just won the League rather than a fifth round Cup tie. They were just not used to winning fifth round Cup ties.

The special train home was a curious one, as it was supposed to provide some kind of disco facility. It turned out to be an empty carriage with no music, but nobody cared. NUFC can party without music, especially after a triumph, and they all felt that this party was going to take them to that elusive trophy. Celebrations took place all the way back home, and for some odd reason, toilet rolls were hurled out of the windows when the train crossed the viaduct in Chester-le-Street, in some kind of ritual. United were back.

Then came Nottingham Forest. *Remember Nottingham Forest,* as the song goes. All of that generation remember this quarter-final, and later ones probably know all about it too. Some have forgotten the match before that game. The club were not used to organising tickets for such a momentous game. To be fair, they could not have really anticipated the scenes which surrounded the scramble for tickets which took place one very cold March night. The gates on Barrack Road were supposed to open at 9.00am on the morning to allow orderly queues to buy the gold-dust. Inevitably, by midnight orderly queues had long since been replaced by total chaos.

Brian and Geordie had arrived about 9.00pm the previous day, and as the night had

worn on, the road resembled something like
some kind of anti-Vietnam demonstration or Paris
protests from the 1960s. At one point, the nearby
allotment crees were dismantled in search of
wood so that fires could be lit to provide much-
needed warmth for the freezing Geordie hordes.

Towards 8.00am or so, the police decided
that something had to be done, and the gates
were opened to allow some of the mob inside the
stadium area. This naturally led to a stampede of
buffalo proportions. The cunning village pair
managed to crawl, climb, jump, and run their way
towards the entrance. They got through a gap,
and returned home with tickets in pockets.
Behind them they left broken flasks, provided by
their Mams.

The match the following week had
everything. A packed St James, huge anticipation,
anxiety, despair, hope, euphoria, and then
afterwards, some disappointment when it was
confirmed that it would have to be played again -
another uneventful day at the Geordie Cathedral.
United went 3-1 down, with centre half Paddy
Howard sent off, a bloke on the pitch with his
trousers down grappling with the police, soon to
be followed by some of the Leazes heading
towards the Forest fans. Some took a detour and
tried to attack a couple of Nottingham players.
The referee took the teams off, brought them
back on, United scored three, and it was time for
the semis. That was until the FA ordered a replay.
There were in fact two replays, on neutral
grounds, before Supermac finally saw off Forest.

Next stop came Hillsbrough. Supermac,
with the help of Terry Hibbitt's exquisite left foot,

blasted Burnley out of the water. The mighty
open Kop swayed, and the Sheffield skies echoed
to the sound of the Geordie roar. Geordie himself
was sitting with Big Micky and the Washington
lads, but Kev and Brian were on the open terrace.
The latter's memory of Supermac's second goal is
slightly blurred, and only constant watching of it
on video helps him to remember at least
something of it. This was mainly due to the fact
that Kev jumped on him, sending him flying onto
the concrete ground. With others in a similar
plight, Brian managed to get up with some
difficulty, and with a mild concussion. Nobody
cared. That bus journey back was brilliant. The
journey to the Final - and Glory - was under way.

The preparation for the anticipated
Wembley triumph seemed to involve a strategy of
packing in the league completely, and just turning
up to pick up the Cup. Neither the team, nor the
fans, seemed to remember that the opposition
was a very mighty Liverpool side under Bill
Shankly. Preparations back in the village involved
the painting of a massive sheet in black and
white. It took an enormous amount of effort, and
paint, and it was hung affectionately out to dry
over the backyard wall. Before setting off for
London, there was one other Cup final to be
tackled. Although league form was now
disastrous, the Texaco Cup was lifted in front of
36,000 fans, with Supermac – again – and Bobby
Moncur – again - doing the job. Brian and some
of the others had been at St James back in the
October watching a 1-1 draw with Morton in that
competition, along with 12,000 hardy souls. One
cup under the belt, and now it was time for the

Big One.

Brian, another Brian, Geordie, and Kev, met up at the Central to catch one of the overnight specials. One bloke stood with a placard near the famous old Clock in the station, with the sign offering £80 for a ticket. No chance, and he was probably still there the next morning, poor bugger. They all arrived in London on the early Saturday morning, borrowed a bottle of milk or two from some posh doorsteps, and arrived in Trafalgar Square. They bumped into Gordon the FishShopOwner, and gave him a couple of cans of Tartan, which he graciously accepted, or rather grabbed. Another offering for all those years of extra chips and match lifts.

After hours of singing and drinking, it was kick-off time - and kick-in-the-face time as well. The match was a total disaster, a humiliation watched by millions of TV viewers, including a despondent Mam and brother Dave back in the old council house. Mr Shankly, and a certain Kevin Keegan, demolished United. There were only three victories that day for the Mags. Brendan Foster won a pre-match race, the National Anthem and Jimmy Hill were drowned out by the noise of the fans, and the Scousers were drowned out by the NUFC.

There were also two major arguments. One had focused upon that massive, heavy sheet. The group argued about whose turn it was to carry it, and it was finally dumped at the end of the match. The other row was between Brian and Geordie. Geordie wanted to stay behind, which, to his credit, he did and continued to sing his head off along with so many other Mags. Brian regrets telling his mate that he just wanted to get out of the bloody place. He had sung for a short while as Liverpool paraded the Cup, but shamefully left long before his mate.

They all met up later in the West End, and the Mags sang themselves hoarse. This was also one of the first occasions when Brian began to take a dislike to some of the Red Scousers, an emotion which was to develop over the years. One, with a Red & White cowboy hat on his head, popped into a bar full of NUFC, and told them all to cheer up, it was only a laugh. His immediate exit indicated that, despite myths to the contrary, the Scouse sense of humour is not always well-timed, or the best in the world.

The journey back was depressing. The other Brian was ordered to climb down from his chosen sleeping berth, the luggage rack above. On the advice of the others, he reluctantly did so. He got his revenge on those London coppers years later, when he spent an evening with the Met at an army barracks in Yorkshire. He was on Territorial Army duty, and the Cockneys were buying free drinks all night, boasting about how much money they were making from the Miners' Strike. The other Brian accepted their hospitality, smiled, spoke rarely, and certainly did not mention that his day job – or lack of it – was that of a striking miner. He just smiled.

Back from that journey in 1974, another task had to be completed. The Wembley job was far from over. Another tradition had to be fulfilled, namely, The Homecoming. Thousands upon thousands turned out on that Monday night on the streets leading towards town, in the town, and for some, in the ground as well. A plastic FA Cup appeared from somewhere, the ground sang to the rafters, and Bobby Moncur appeared on TV, distraught and tearful. That team were all genuinely ashamed, and Joe Harvey was overcome with emotion.

The fans felt no shame, of course. They were doing their duty, showing their loyalty, and listening to the apologies, which it has to be stressed, were heartfelt and sincere, unlike some others muttered on similar occasions in the future.

Chapter Nine

Another wedding & two goodbyes

Another season had to be faced, and Kev, Brian, Geordie, brother Dave, and all the rest had to pick themselves up off the floor. Naturally they did. The Joe Harvey team never really did however, although revenge of a sort was extracted against Liverpool in a home match in late winter when United hammered them 4–1. Brian enjoyed that one, but another Brian with the same surname got their goal. That surname was to haunt him in years to come. That day of revenge was short-lived, as a month later Liverpool put four goals in at Anfield, without reply from the Black & White opposition - apart from the Mags in the Anfield Road end, who, as was the tradition, out-sang the Kop. The season ended in a lowly 15th position.

Some away games stood out during this spell, but not always because of events on the pitch. One was in November, when Brian was very fortunate to be playing in midfield one Saturday morning at Usworth Comp in Washington: very fortunate, as he would normally have caught the same train down to Boro as Kev and Geordie. He was to join them later, but never did. Whilst he watched the match, and took in the infamous Boro Bottle Run afterwards – the locals were usually keen to offer that post-match welcome to the railway station – he was unaware that his two mates had spent the afternoon in a Smoggie hospital. They had arrived early in Middlesbrough, drank copious amounts of beer and whisky with a set of Mags, entered the NUFC end, and shouted, for a laugh, that *Boro Boys, We Are Here, Oh, Oh, Oh*. Colleagues did not instantly recognise the joke, and they were immediately dispatched to the hospital.

Geordie, badly bruised and with eyes becoming darker by the minute, was particularly frustrated, as Kev seemed to get more attention from the nursing staff due to his extremely pale look. Geordie knew from experience that Kev's pallid complexion had nothing to do with his medical condition, and everything to do with the results of over-consumption of alcohol. Brian knocked on Geordie's door on the Sunday night on his way up to the local club disco, only for Jessie, his Mam, to suggest that he should come inside and see if his Mag mate was coming out. This was odd, as club discos on a Sunday night were normally the highlight of a very dull social calendar. Geordie's eyes were now extremely black, but in true, stubborn manner, he put on a pair of sunglasses, and his jacket, and climbed up the hill to the normal venue. This caused some bewilderment amongst both the NUFC and the SAFC, as sunglasses were not usual wear at that time of the year.

Another away match at Leeds in March saw a useful 1-1 draw, but nearly saw Kev, Geordie, and Brian landing in the canal. The Geordie Army piled out of the railway station, ready as always for the battle with their hooligan rivals. For once, a sensible decision, at least in theory, was made. The three decided to leave the troops, and chose a more tranquil path towards Elland Road, so they could meet up in a pub where Mags were in full occupation. As they strolled near the canal, they were spotted by a large group of Leeds thugs. Brian used his increasingly talkative skills, looked for the leader, always the right thing to do, and engaged with him. He pointed out that the Army was in the main street, and the leader seemed to agree, feeling that it would be a waste of valuable time attacking these Mags. Unfortunately, he did not have total command of some of his squad, and it was time to curl up in a ball. It is difficult to hear much in such a position, but Brian was alarmed at one comment, as the kicks rained in, which involved speculation upon whether these Geordies could swim. Fortunately, this was never tested, and they left the three on the ground, bruised and battered.

The trio recovered, made it to the match to see the draw, and noticed the same squad right next to the NUFC end, baiting and taunting throughout the game. Ten minutes from the end, a set of Geordies visited them, and Brian admits that he felt a sense of justice had been done, but he did hope that the Leader survived. At least that Leeds thug had tried to call his pack off at the canal.

Another momentous event occurred in 1975, and it clashed with a would-be FA Cup run. Brother Dave took his wedding vows as the Mags took off for Walsall in the fourth round. The previous round had gone well, with a 2-0 away win at Manchester City, with goals from Micky

Burns and Geoff Nulty. The atmosphere down there was hostile, as the City and United fans exchanged pleasantries, and just about everything else, in the Kippax End. Brian, Geordie, and some others, avoided missiles and enjoyed a splendid victory.

After the match they found themselves at Victoria railway station, and they were isolated. One bloke approached them and asked for the time. This was an old trick in those violent days to test out an accent. The response was immediate, and he was placed onto the ground. Only on this occasion, Brian was slightly bemused, pointing out that this bloke had not looked like a hooligan. One of the lads said he was not taking any chances, and they jumped on a train. To this day, there must be a man in Manchester who wants Newcastle to lose every match they ever play, perhaps even against his rivals in that city. He probably bought a watch that night as well.

Soon, it was Wedding Day. For once, Geordie was anxious about a game for non-football reasons. He confided that he was worried about telling brother Dave that he had to refuse the wedding invitation. Obviously, he had to go to Walsall for the cup-tie. Brian laughed, as did brother Dave when he heard the news. Naturally, it was understood that the cup commitment had to come first. Brian was not allowed that choice, and attended the ceremony. Fr Joe, a Red & White priest, married the couple. The priest did not stay for the obligatory shaking of hands afterwards, but jumped into his car with his sister Teresa. The SAFC had a home game, and some of the Mag guests gesticulated at Fr Joe as he took off from the car park with his Red & White scarf hanging out of his window. They were joking – just.

The wedding party trooped off for the reception, with Dad wearing a flaired suit borrowed from his son. He had spent his own suit money on a horse, and as usual, the donkey had lost. At one point, nobody was bothered if he came anyway, but Mam relented, and asked brother Dave to lend him one of his suits. This explains Dad's appearance, looking for all the world like an old Hampstead Heath gay playwright.

Meanwhile, down in the West Midlands, Geordie and Newcastle United were having a mare, plunging out of the Cup against the lower league opposition. News of the defeat reached the disco on the night. On the Sunday night, Geordie appeared, muttering that he might as well have gone to the bloody wedding instead. The season was effectively over, but there was more to come in early summer. This was the end of an era, as Joe Harvey was forced to say goodbye as manager after so many years of loyal service to the club he loved as much as the fans. Joe's days had been numbered for quite a while, and he was replaced by Gordon Lee. More of him later, except there was the usual optimism that another new dawn was on the horizon.

Lee seemed to come across as determined and professional, although he did alarm fans when he stated that he did not want any stars in his teams. Newcastle United without a couple of stars to worship? In August, brother Dave and Brian were in the Paddock, for some strange reason, and were privileged enough to see one of those heroes score one of the best goals of his career against Leicester in a home 3-0 victory. Supermac rates it as one of his best ever goals. That says a lot.

As Joe Harvey left that summer, Brian too had to say goodbye. He was leaving the North East to live elsewhere, although, naturally, he was not saying goodbye to the club.

Chapter Ten

Exile in Liverpool

Brian's A-Level results were due in August 1975, and he was optimistic. The sixth form had proved far more productive than his previous years at that school in Mackem City. His O-Level performance two years earlier had been quite shaky, and his main source of pride in those examinations had been his leading role in the failure of most of his class to be registered as being able to speak English. They all faced an English oral test, and Brian and SAFC Kev had arranged for their mates, including Kev, Jess, and Jim, to speak in broad Geordie/Durham dialect. It counted for only 5% of the paper, and some of the group were totally affronted that they had to prove that they could speak the nation's language. The angry school Head demanded an enquiry. He was furious that most of his top class could speak French, Spanish, and even Latin, but somehow were recorded as being unable to speak English.

A-levels were a different matter, and Brian's studies picked up. Exams finished, while Gordon Lee prepared for the 1975 season, Brian spent a week as a gardener for the newsagent, and the rest of the summer as a gardener for Hetton Council. It should be added that Brian did not have, and still does not have, any gardening skills, but occasionally he was let loose on grass-cutting equipment. In early August, Brian phoned his Mam from a telephone box which actually worked and was not vandalised, just outside Eppleton pit. She expressed her joy at the results, and by October, village life was over, and City life was beginning – in Liverpool!

In retrospect, Brian's choice of university was a foolish mistake. That 1974 FA Cup Final should have been a warning what life amongst the Red Scousers would be like. He had missed a trick. Those early days in academia were dominated by an overwhelming homesickness, something he had not felt since the age of nine when he was forced to go on some daft camping expedition in West Durham, without a football in sight. Then, he was homesick only because he was worried about what was happening back in the troubled home, but on this occasion the reason for his feeling was very different.

University was a world away from life in a Durham pit village, like another planet. Brian felt he spoke a different language, which he did of course, and that he was from a different world, which he was, of course. The second night summed it up. Brian was talking to a posh lad from Nottingham, and asked him whether he supported Forest or County. The reply was ominous. He did not like "soccer", but would not mind a game of chess. A couple of days onwards, Brian felt he now had two choices. One, *Run For Home,* as Geordie folk-rock band Lindisfarne advised, or just stick it all out, concentrate upon away games – after all, that was one of the reasons he was there in the first place – and get home to as many games as possible.

And then, as so often happens in life, like

begins to meet like. He bumped into Baz, later known as Fat Baz, a loud and bigoted Blackburn fan. Sid turned up, a solid Brummie and West Brom supporter, along with Clive, a southerner who followed Liverpool, but he can be forgiven for that as he was good fun. Fat Baz and Brian were slightly baffled that both Sid and Clive had another team each, namely Chelsea and Crystal Palace, but this mattered little. Football talk was on the agenda, as was socialising, well, drinking actually. Tim, a Southend fan, emerged, along with Barney, York City. The latter would be the future husband of Brian's first wife, Jane, and his son Tom was also to be his godson. Naturally, his spiritual welfare was duly attended to, and Tom is a fanatical United fan to this day, even though he now has to watch games from Shanghai most of the time due to job location.

Back to the formation of the group in that hall of residence in Liverpool. There were women as well, which again was a considerable bonus. Janet from Guernsey amused a Geordie collection one night when she said, sincerely, that she never thought Geordies attended universities. Anne was from Stafford, and Julie was an American on a Junior Year Abroad scheme from her own university in Tulane, New Orleans. She was to become a very major player on Brian's scene in the coming months. It was all looking up after all, as this was no middle class hellhole. Others would later turn up too, including SAFC Jess from schooldays, and Pete the Cockney, a Michael Caine-type character and Arsenal fan. He seemed to regard Mags as totally mad, as he had encountered them at one match at Highbury on a previous occasion.

Beyond Liverpool, Kev was at Aston in Birmingham, along with a new, and vital NUFC man, Gus from Leam Lane. He was a very bright scientist, and extremely interested in football and women, most of the time anyway. It has to be stated that on one future occasion, he refused to get out of bed for a match at West Brom. Kev took his Geordie guests, including Brian, over to the game, whilst Gus recovered from his hangover in time for a party on the night. As university days advanced, there were even Geordie Societies formed, which involved cultural visits, mainly to matches actually. There is some truth in the rumour that Mike Elliott, the comedian and later radio broadcaster, was promised decent accommodation by Kev at one of their events, only to find himself sleeping on the floor. Knowing Mike, he was probably not bothered.

There was so much to do in the process of readjustment away from life back home, or rather away from St James. Regular information arrived every Tuesday morning via a parcel from Mam, which included a letter, and the Football Pink, such a vital source of news for exiled Mags across Britain and the world. Sadly and tragically, the Pink finally folded many years later, unable to compete with the lack of games on Saturdays, the age of mobile pictures and the rest. That last Pink is a valuable item, and Brian is not alone in keeping it in his drawer. The Pink was more than just a footy paper. It was a lifeline for exiles across the world. It was part of the culture.

Away games now took over in the autumn of 1975. As always, a couple stand out,

for different reasons. One involved the arrival of
brother Dave and Geordie at the hall of residence
one late Friday afternoon for a game at Stoke.
They had an altercation with some Scousers on
the evening, and Geordie nearly missed a free
breakfast on the Saturday morning. Under very
strict orders from Brian to say nothing, bacon and
eggs were ordered in the canteen, only for
Geordie to remark loudly that he could not
believe that his mate got such good food.
Fortunately, the woman serving was slightly deaf,
and he sat down unquestioned and unnoticed.

They set off for Stoke, teamed up with Kev who
had travelled north from Birmingham, and
predictably, Stoke was not very welcoming.
Gowling, complete with that degree which
impressed Gordon Lee, earned United a 1-1 draw.
After the match, the slow train journey back to
Derby was not a calm one, given the number of
Stoke fans travelling on it, and the darts incident
is perhaps best left unmentioned. It was also a
relief to see some rather infamous NUFC on the
platform at Derby as well.

      The other match brought a tinge of
homesickness for Brian. It was the annual trip to
Leeds.   United went down 3-0, and his mood
went down as well, partly because of the result,
but mainly because he had to leave Leeds railway
station heading south to Liverpool. The Geordie
masses were naturally heading north, and he
wished he was going in that direction. It was soon
time to go home for Christmas. On Boxing Day he
left for Burnley for a cracking day out, although
Mam did not seem to mind. She was used to all
this. It was also time for home games as well.

Early January witnessed a 5-0 slaughter of the
Blue Scousers, although not all five goals were
actually witnessed by Brian, Gordon, and
Geordie. In fact, brother Dave did not see any of
them. They had all arrived late from the Printers
Pie, a favourite venue in that era, famous for its
high quality Exhibition beer. The group took an
extra Exhibition, and thus missed the first goal.

      Brother Dave's achievement in missing
the rest mainly involved the Gallowgate End
toilets. All former residents of that part of the
ground will recall that there was a certain
difficulty in getting up to, or down to and back up
from, those bogs, with their surrounding trees and
shrubbery. The club was not in the business of
providing luxurious access to luxurious toilets.
Dave was not the sort to take the alternative
course, chosen by some, and just unzip his flies
on the spot, at least not at home matches anyway.
He was trying to get down to, or back up from,
the said toilets, as the goals rained in. The group
gathered at the back, and headed down the steps
to beat the bus queues, which were horrific, only
for the last goal to find the net.

Chapter Eleven

Two Cups & three bruised ribs

But brother Dave would soon see the goals which were to send him and the NUFC nation into euphoria. Brian had left for Liverpool after the Everton game, but was only there for three days, before he landed in London with thousands of United supporters for the League Cup semi-final first leg at White Hart Lane. Kev found himself in the wrong toilet at half time – bogs again – and returned with a sore head, given to him by a Spurs fan. United lost 1-0, but sore heads were around again on the following Wednesday, for very different reasons. It was celebration time, as the crowd roared their side on to a 3-1 victory.

As the group, including brother Dave, stood right behind the Gallowgate net, they saw an ashen-faced Pat Jennings, the very experienced Tottenham goalkeeper, who seemed intimidated by the noise blasting up to the sky. Keegan later felt his first goal at St James in 1982 was sucked in by the fans. Certainly, this was the case in Alan Gowling's opener on that scintillating night which put Newcastle through to this Final.

Attention quickly turned to the other Cup, the Lady from Hell, and they all travelled down to Coventry for the fourth round tie on the Saturday. Tim, the Southend fan from university, fancied going, but failed to realise just what an away cup-tie entailed. He and Brian met up with Kev, Gus, brother Dave, and some Shiney Mags. At one point before the game, a policewoman sitting on a horse, responding to one of the group's lewd remarks, suggested that he probably wished he was the horse instead, which managed to shut him up. Tim meanwhile was enjoying himself, drinking at the same speed as the rest, and impressed some by eating a raw onion as it rolled out of some local vegetable shop. He missed the entire match, as he slept against a barrier in the away end. United earned a useful draw to take Coventry back up to the North East, hammering them 5-0 in the replay.

February took in the fifth round. Cup fever was back in town, and in Julie's tiny bedroom in Liverpool where Brian usually resided. His romance and NUFC life was blossoming at the same time, and Julie wanted to experience the latter for herself. She soon realised the importance of the game early Saturday morning, as, despite her best efforts, Brian's sexual drive seemed to disappear. He had other things on his mind. Tim, unsurprisingly, felt he had experienced enough, so the train set off from Merseyside without him, but with Julie, and Janet from Guernsey. Brian spotted a fellow Mag, Ged, who was a student from Wallsend, and total fanatic.

The same Ged reappeared many years later, having written "Fifty Years of Hurt." No prizes for guessing what that book was about.

As they waited for Geordie, brother Dave, and Big Micky at Bolton railway station, a special train rumbled into the platform. Janet expressed surprise at the decorated windows – she could only see eyes peering through piled-up beer cans. The small Bolton welcoming party wisely left, and the group headed off into town. 17,000 Mags were there that day, and Julie, who studied in New Orleans back in the USA, said it was better than the Mardi Gras. The vast hordes assembled and swayed on the huge open terrace in the ground, and saw a pulsating 3-3 draw, which earned a home replay, always enough in the Cup. Two main memories remain of that day. The first was the sight of Supermac lashing in a piledriver which sent the away Kop into ecstasy. The second was the impact of the piledriver.

Big Micky and the others had tried their best to protect Julie and Janet from the surges during the game, but in the chaos, the American guest was sent flying down the terraces. After the match, as she sat on the train back to Scouse City, she was clearly in agony, and Brian took her from Lime Street railway station directly to the hospital. The diagnosis was three very badly bruised ribs, and a subsequent overnight stay in hospital. Unbeknown to Brian, Gus and Kev were in trouble too, as their Geordie Society van had failed to start after the match and was subsequently dumped. They were then chased by some locals, and reached the sanctuary of the near-empty Bolton station. The only lad with them without a Geordie accent responded when asked the time- the old trick - by a group of dodgy characters. Fortunately, Gus overheard and spoke up immediately. They were Mags and the strays immediately put their colours back on, having narrowly escaped an attack from a group of Geordies.

Meanwhile, Brian's emotions further south on Merseyside were mixed. The joy and exhilaration, the mass hysteria experienced at Bolton, was yet another one of those days when life with NUFC was near-heaven. They could let the fans down a hundred times, but such occasions, along with the League Cup semi triumph, simply made up for it all.

On the other hand, the first proper romantic love of his life was in real pain, and his guilt was obvious. By the Sunday afternoon, Julie was lying in her sick-bed in the tiny flat. Brian took on a nurturing, caring role, and bought her flowers and chocolate, although those purchases were on the advice of one of the other lasses. Julie was impressed at his devotion, until the Tuesday night that is. For once, Brian was anxious about a match for very different reasons, Sheepishly, he sat next to Julie's bed that night, and informed her that he would probably not be back until Thursday or possibly Friday. This, after previous days of twenty-four hour care. He added that he had to go up for the replay.

To this day, Julie probably does not quite understand what a replay actually is, but seemed to understand why her lover had to go to it. She was crestfallen, but she recovered, and the romance survived. So did the FA Cup run. The match at St James was a 0-0 draw, but United finally saw off Bolton at neutral Elland Road in Leeds, with Ged, the Wallsend lad from university, in attendance.

Life was certainly packed with action in those winter months, and study was rarely on the agenda. How could it be, with concentration

focused upon two Cup runs and a new girlfriend?
There was also a certain League away match to
attend before the League Cup Final trip, which
involved a journey of about three miles to Anfield.
The Red Scousers won 2-0 - nothing new about
that. The Geordies outsang the Kop, and nothing
new about that either. The latter offered *You'll
Never Walk Alone* a couple of times, after they had
scored of course, whilst the Anfield Road end
rocked to the sound of *Blaydon Races* and the full
NUFC songbook.

      A curious incident occurred beforehand
in the Arkle pub, which was packed with United
fans. One took exception to Clive's presence, as
he was wearing a Liverpool scarf. Brian
intervened only to be told that he was not a
proper Geordie, with his Durham accent, and a
brief scuffle broke out. Clive looked on bemused.
As a Liverpool fan, he was an exception, as he
never boasted and mocked Newcastle.

      All the rest did, and wondered why
Geordies had no sense of humour. This is easily
explained. When a Scouser constantly repeats
they live in the greatest city in the world, have the
greatest sense of humour in the world, and the
greatest team in the world, it begins to grate if
heard on a daily basis. Add the fact that Brian's
first name and surname was the same as their
right-winger's, which meant he got the same stuff
every time he had to give his name to somebody,
his growing dislike of the Red half of the city was
increasing.

      The defeat at Liverpool did not matter.
There were other fish to fry at the end of that
February month: Manchester City at Wembley.

The train down was quick and full of hope, the train back was slow and full of despair. Brian had a spare ticket, as brother Dave had fallen ill, and his younger sibling intended to sell it at a profit in order to clear some of the overdraft off which was growing rapidly because of life with NUFC. He bumped into a lass dressed in Black & White outside the ground, and sold it at face value. True, she was attractive, but this was not his motivation. He could not sell a ticket to a Mag comrade for profit, and all proper members of the tribe feel the same. No exploitation of your brothers or sisters, he thought - leave that to the Board.

The match itself was lost 2-1. Denis Tueart, a Geordie, scored, and plummeted further down in Scotty's opinion, which, as the book opening mentioned, was already low after he tried to show him Sunderland's FA Cup trophy back in Walker in 1973. The group left Wembley gutted, but at least this time it had not been a public humiliation. That eased the pain only slightly, and Brian again had that feeling that he was travelling in the wrong direction as he caught the train to Liverpool whilst the rest headed up home. He sought out a crowd of mates who would not mock the defeat, and managed to avoid any Scousers or Manchester City fans for the night. By early March, the flirtation with the other Cup was over too. Kev, Gus, and the others watched the team go down at Derby. Expectations had been lowered anyway, as half the team had already gone down with flu before the match.

The Gallowgate curse had struck again. It would continue to do so in later years as well.

Chapter Twelve

To Highbury & not New York

Surprisingly, against this hectic background of home and away match travel, the romance with Julie was intensifying, and Brian found solace in it. He still followed the club, but a large part of his devotion turned towards the American, which helped him to recover from the tribulations of two Cup exits. Glorious months were spent together, in the west of Ireland, where they spent many a night of passion in b&bs, turning around huge portraits of Jesus and Our Lady on the walls. The lovers were both lapsed Catholics. They also took in the Lakes where, due to bad planning, they passed one night camping on a rubbish tip. It was dark and Brian could not see the surroundings properly.

The couple visited Washington, Washington County Durham that is, and not the other one in the USA which was her home town. During the summer, he showed her the ground, naturally, and Whitley Bay, where a drunken bloke overheard she was from Washington and told her that he used to work at a pit there.

In late July Julie had to return home, and Brian was left cutting the grass again in Hetton-le-Hole. They planned to see each other in the USA at Christmas, but Brian never made it across the Pond. Instead, he was watching Paul Cannell and Alan Kennedy putting two goals past the SAFC over that festive period. Despite Brian's letters, Julie rarely kept in touch, but astonishingly expressed sorrow when Brian told her two days before the scheduled flight that he was not going. Barney consoled him over a pint in the Biddick in Fatfield. Thus ended one love, which brutally coincided with the loss of another love.

In that long hot summer of 1976, Gordon Lee sold Supermac to Arsenal, and there was uproar in the Geordie nation. Supermac was worshipped. To the faithful, he was the Shearer of the 1970s, though not quite as good, which is no insult to Malcolm. He was the standard-bearer of the famous Number 9 shirt and wore it with pride and gusto as he hammered down the pitch with speed and strength. *Supermac, Superstar, How Many Goals Have You Scored So Far?* Lee wanted to complete his team without heroes. His remark about Gowling's degree still rankles amongst some of the crowd. Who needs a bloody degree to play football, for God's Sake? Supermac certainly never had one, but he had a considerable knowledge of the location of the net.

At first, Lee rode the storm. After all, he had taken the side to an FA Cup quarter-final and a League Cup final, and seemed to be forming a top-six side. In October, Brian travelled across to Manchester United for a League Cup game with a couple of fanatics from university, and the match led to the song, *We Hate Man U,' Cos They Beat Us 7-2.* Other reasons for hating Man United would come later. Nobody really remembers, or rather cares too much about that match, and it's only recalled through the song.

However, everybody from that era

remembers, and cares deeply, about a game in early December: Supermac's debut against Newcastle at Highbury. About 10,000 Geordies landed in London for the occasion. Brother Dave and Brian met up in a bar at Kings Cross, whilst Geordie, Big Micky, and the Washington lads were already up in the North London area. They never met up with them, and one of that group apparently spent the afternoon with a Lady of the Night, or of the Day to be more accurate. It turned out to be a wise choice, as Supermac gave Gordon Lee his early Christmas present.

Some of the Mags, including brother Dave and Brian, sang *Supermac's A Two-Faced Bastard, Tra La La La Laa La La La La La,* to that familiar Xmas tune, and *Oh Malcolm, Malcolm, We'll Walk A Mile And A Bit, To Rub Your Face In The Shit, Oh Malcolm.* This latter ditty replaced their old favourite that they would walk a million miles for one of his goals, oh Malcolm. But deep down, they did not really believe it, and knew who the real culprit was. After a disastrous 5-3 defeat, and the inevitable Supermac hat-trick, a small and rather foolish Arsenal mob waited outside to greet the Geordie tribe. The welcome did not last long, as the Cockneys soon realised that it was not appropriate to greet the away following. Brian regretted one incident, but felt justified, as a big Gooner tried to bang him, and he responded with a Glasgow, or rather Shiney, kiss.

Arriving back in Liverpool, Brian met up with Clive, who consoled him, partly because he understood the pain of the Supermac goals, and mainly because he hated Arsenal anyway. He seemed impressed that a Cockney had fallen onto the deck, but this was the least of Brian's concerns – Malcolm had kicked them all in the face, all the NUFC were on the deck, and it was extremely painful. Gordon Lee would not last long. A couple of months later, against a background of serious crowd trouble in the Corner who knew of his imminent departure, United lost to Manchester City 3-1 in the FA Cup. Lee, the man who sold a brilliant centre forward, was leaving for pastures new.

The next day, Lee was off to Everton, supposedly to be near his family, and unfortunately nearer Brian in Merseyside. It was bad enough living there anyway, without having "The Man who Shot Supermac" in charge of the club just over Stanley Park from Anfield.

Things were not going well, on or off the pitch. Brian was living in that area, near to the Liverpool stadium, and far too close to the Scouse heartland. In these two years, he saw the Red Scousers lift the European Cup, partly helped by Alan Kennedy, an ex-Mag, and worse, a Shiney Row lad. These were not great times, and once again Brian encountered the boasting and mockery of the Reds surrounding him. By this stage, he would occasionally go over to Everton, partly because of his resentment of "the greatest fans in the world", and partly because he thought that the Blue Scousers were better fans and of course less successful. He was able to identify with their situation, naturally.

These were not great days for United fans, as chaos was breaking out at the club. United appointed Richard Dinnis against the background of a player revolt, and managed to qualify for Europe, but a bleak horizon awaited, descending into chaos when the hapless manger did not even recognise a player the club had signed from Hearts.

Brian was also trying to recover from the loss of his Scottish Gran. She had always been a sanctuary for him in childhood days, and in his early teens when domestic trauma had sometimes proved too much to handle. After a major nervous breakdown, Brian's Dad had settled down, but his Mam became a cause for concern as she began to suffer from panic attacks. Looking back, this was probably a kind of response, almost a relief, that her own turmoils were no longer around. And as the club struggled, there was of course no Julie around anymore.

These last years at Liverpool University became slightly depressing. No Julie, and only the occasional fling with a couple of Irish lasses. They were complete opposites. Geraldine had taken the pledge not to drink and was from deepest Galway. Marie was from Belfast, and took pledges of a different kind, which did bring some joy. Brian abandoned his principles, as she was a Manc follower, but felt that his decision to accept some of her pledges was justified. Obviously, they never discussed football. At another stage, Fat Baz, the bloody Blackburn fanatic, managed to ruin a potential night of passion with a nurse at a party by barging in the room singing Rovers songs. The moment was lost for her, and passion went pear-shaped for Brian.

It all began to go pear-shaped at Gallowgate as well. Brian travelled up home one autumn to see Bastia in the UEFA Cup, and the fruitless journey disintegrated with the skills of the Dutchman Johnny Rep as he destroyed United. This was not helped by yet another pre-match prediction claiming Rep was past it. In January 1978, as these increasingly miserable university days ended, Brian met some of the Shiney lads at Peterborough for an away cup-tie. He was confronted by one of the southerners who managed to bang him on the head with a full - a full - beer can. Chaos erupted, and Brian was "bitterly" offended. This was Peterborough, not West Ham or Millwall or Leeds. Fortunately, some of the lads intervened. The police intervened also, as some other locals were baiting Mags. This did not last long, and they all went on to see a 1-1 draw, so at least it led to a replay.

Then came the worst away match of Brian's life, with the possible exception of Wigan in the League Cup a couple of decades later: Wrexham. Brian paid Barney a fiver to drive him down there from Liverpool. United had held the mighty Welsh club to 2-2 in the FA Cup tie at St James, and the replay took place on a dark, wet February night in Wales. Cliches are allowed on this one. Wrexham was a very difficult place to get to, but the match was far worse. Thousands of Mags stood behind the goal. The team was under the command of Bill McGarry, the iron disciplinarian who would have been a good Sergeant Major, but was totally useless as a football manager. United lost 4-1, and the soaked Geordies behind the goal justifiably let loose a torrent of abuse at the side. They had sung their hearts out, until they realised that most of the

team could not care less. Brian still believes that
Bill McGarry owes him a fiver for that trip.

Ironically, it was left to Blyth Spartans to
defend the region's honour in front of a capacity
crowd at St James in the next round. Northern
League Spartans had drawn at Wrexham, robbed
of the win they deserved only because of a
bizarre refereeing decision. Kev and Gus
represented the Mag element, amongst others, at
the first game in North Wales. The police were
totally unprepared for the massive away
following, and Gus went berserk when the Welsh
were allowed to take a corner again when the flag
fell down after the first corner kick had been
cleared. Wrexham scored from it, towards the last
minute of the game. Afterwards, the Kev and Gus
narrowly escaped an ambush by the Welsh in the
process. Nevertheless, the draw gave Blyth the
honour of being the only non-league side to make
the quarter-final draw, in which they were paired
with Arsenal.

Whilst the packed St James turned up to
cheer on Spartans, the 42,000 crowd including
some Shiney SAFC who thus found unity with the
NUFC. Brian sat in his house in Anfield listening
to that replay back in the North East, jumping
around, pacing, and generally going bananas. It
was all to no avail, as Blyth failed to overcome the
Welsh giants by an odd goal.   At least the
amateurs gave it a damn good go, unlike their
more illustrious neighbours in the North East
regional capital. McGarry and the Board finished
the job in the league, and at the end of the season
Newcastle were duly relegated.

All Mags agreed, which in itself is a rare

event, as there are usually a wide variety of opinions. They were following a club with second-rate players, a second-rate manager, and above all, an exceptionally second-rate Board.

Chapter Thirteen

Back down & back home

By the summer of 1978, Brian was grateful to leave Scouse City for good. In later decades there were occasional returns to watch the Mags or just pass through on his way to Dublin to catch the boat, to see Fr Steve or on a romantic weekend with a girlfriend. He took his Gap Year in Gateshead, at the National Carriers goods distribution centre. Given that the option of exploring the Amazon or walking across China was unavailable, it seemed a sensible choice, and it paid good money.

He then moved onto some work with the Wordsworth Museum, spending most of his time at the Newcastle University end of the operation. The boss was obsessed with the documents of Wordsworth and his circle, and thought football was a waste of time. He was not alone in thinking that, but this did stop some good football talk with one colleague, Ian from Leeds, who seemed to understand the blow which had hit the Newcastle fan.

Brian started off on an MA course in Newcastle at the same time as another United fan, Alan Milburn, who obviously had a famous surname and later emerged in a New Labour Government. The course soon turned into a PhD route. Some of the old crowd of Mags had departed further afield. Kev disappeared, ending

up in Philadelphia, the US version that is. Fr Steve
had gone too. Converting to the priesthood after
voluntary work in Pakistan, he ended up in Perth,
Australia. He worked in a hospice out there, and
initially managed to hide his faith and day job
from a football team he played for. They were of
Glaswegian orange stock. Fr Steve naturally
retained his NUFC faith. He had no choice in that,
and was kept informed of events back home via
his Mam, Monica, and the brothers, Mick and
Paul.

Meanwhile, new United fans entered Brian's life,
particularly in the village, with Sam, Mogga, and
yet another Brian, who was destined to be the
chair of the local NUM in the Massive Struggle
with Thatcher in 1984.

Sam was a tremendous character, very
calm and easy-going, unless talking about United.
In fact, he was so calm that he had to be knocked
out of bed for matches - home ones that is, not
away. Mogga loved to sing his NUFC repertoire,
particularly if one of his best mates Lofty, a SAFC,
was within hearing range. Those two always got
on well, most of the time. A quiz night out
celebration saw the team disintegrate into a row
over football, caused by that pair, and led to a
rapid departure from a Chinese restaurant in
Chester-le-Street. After bitter experience, Brian
learned to keep a girlfriend from Newcastle well
away from them. A night in the back of the car on
the disused railway line was always under threat
if Mogga saw the couple in a local pub for a pre-
car drink. There is a time and place for constant
NUFC singing, which was Mogga's forte.

Lyn too emerged, living with SAFC Min,

and she later won the argument about the future football allegiance of their first child. It caused considerable tension, but all knew that the bairn would be black and white, everybody except Min that is.

At St James, United had now plunged into the old Division 2. Some of the songs stand out far more than the games themselves. The Geordies still followed the team away, now to even less exotic venues. They would gather and sing *Weh Ya Kna, Weh Ya Kna*, or *Kiss My Arse, My Arse, We're Geordies, We're Fucking Thick, Kiss My Arse, My Arse*. This was obviously some kind of ritual of defiance, as most of the players on the pitch provided little entertainment, let alone defiance.

Few games that season stand out, but the visit to Cambridge in September 1978 certainly does. It was a trip to the medieval and modern day home of Britain's elite. The Geordie elite set off in a rather confused manner. Brian and Geordie were having their last pint in the Bird in Hand on the Friday night, after an exciting night out in the club playing cards and dominoes. Paul breezed in, and asked them if they fancied piling into the van to Cambridge. This they did, picking up their coats from their Mams' houses and telling them that they would be back by Sunday. As always, Mams did not flicker. It involved NUFC travel and no further questions were asked. Questions were asked in the van, as for some inexplicable reason it ended up near Nottingham in the middle of the night. Paul had taken the wrong route. A major row erupted, only quelled by some cans of beer, and the lads all went back

to sleep. They landed in Cambridge towards
10.00am, and by 11.00am had managed to buy
some more cans of beer.

Cambridge was not exactly prepared for
the arrival of a couple of thousand Mags. There
were punts on the River Cam, and by lunchtime
United fans were jumping into the little river,
landing alongside the upper class punters. Visiting
Japanese tourists took photographs, thinking it
was some bizarre kind of ritual. Those Far Eastern
visitors must have taken them back to Japan and
told friends in Tokyo, or wherever, that they had
witnessed a typical Cambridge carnival.

*Cambridge: Newcastle fans jump in River Cam as
Japanese tourists snap this ancient British ritual*

Typical it was not. Geordie managed to
get thrown out of the ground twice, as the local
police did not like his singing, and he retired to

the van. Mick managed to drop the smuggled
bottle of wine onto the terraces. In search of food,
Jackie tried to climb into the hamburger stand at
the back of the United end. The burger bar shut
rapidly as the staff looked on in horror at the
hungry Geordies surrounding them. On the pitch,
the team managed a 0-0 draw in a very dull
match, whilst Geordie spent the afternoon in the
van, which turned out to be the better option.

Afterwards, it was decided that
Huntingdon was well worth a visit. They all
arrived there, slightly bedraggled and looking
very much like they did not come from the Home
Counties. Jacky livened up one quiet pub lounge
with his famous serenading act. This involved
playing a non-existent guitar, singing old Dean
Martin love songs, to any unsuspecting couple.
Back home, everybody used to enjoy this act, but
the pair sitting in the corner seemed distinctly
unamused, and clearly thought he was a little
strange. The subsequent visit to a nightclub
produced little more success, as it ended up in an
altercation with a very large Chelsea fan, and a
rapid exit from the said night club. Paul was
sitting in the van, prepared to move as soon as his
fellow travellers were ready. They were. They
arrived back in the region on the Sunday
morning, absolutely knackered, but pleased that
they had been to a NUFC away match.

Another away match during those early
days in the Second Division remains in the
memory of Brian, Geordie, and Gus. With little
early season optimism, they caught the train via
Carlisle for an evening at Deepdale, the ground of
Preston North End, and United lost 1-0. Early

optimism was shaken, but the group were soon to be shaking, literally. A decision was made similar to the one at Leeds which had nearly led to a visit into that canal in Yorkshire. They decided to stay behind for a quick pint, let the angry Geordie army head off, and then catch the next train up to Carlisle for the planned night-club visit. After all, Preston was hardly Leeds.

Leaving the pub, Gus spotted a young local following the group, noting that he had clearly overheard their accents. Action was taken immediately, and the youngster ran off. Unfortunately, as Gus pointed out, when they approached the station, the young follower was back. Within seconds, he shouted across the road to a 60-strong group of Preston supporters. Quite a large number, so it might have well just have been Leeds anyway. The result was the same, and it was again time to curl up in a ball. A steel comb was used in self-defence, but not much else, as the four were battered until the police came out of the station. They intervened, and in very Anglo-Saxon words, told them to get off the ground, and head back to Newcastle.

Then came a very emotional moment in the Black & White life of Brian as they stood in Carlisle station. His hand was swelling like a balloon, and it was decided that he had to get up to the hospital. The others believed that he needed company, which was very touching. Only, they added that a coin should be tossed just to see who should accompany him, as there was a night club to be visited. Geordie lost, sat in the hospital totally disgruntled about missing the night out, and muttering that a Big Club should not have to play against Preston anyway. Brian was diagnosed with a badly-broken hand along with some bruises, and left with a plaster. Gus, who had of course won the toss, joined the group of skinheads whom they had met on the train and thoroughly enjoyed himself in that night club, much to Geordie's annoyance.

It was not a good start to the season, but a combination of Sunderland hooligans and a penalty shoot-out were about to complete a bad fortnight for him. Brian's birthday on August 29th saw a 2-2 draw away at Roker Park, with Cartwright, ex-Blyth Spartans, and Davies getting the goals. That was the good news. The bad had occurred on the previous Friday night, as Brian was travelling back from Mackem City after a night out with SAFC Kev and his mates. Sitting at the back of the bus, two young villagers shouted down to him, asking how many Mags would be at the first leg of the League Cup derby. Brian, in the middle of the bus, looked back and indicated that silence was essential, as the bus had not yet left the Pennywell area. It was too late. A particularly brave bloke looked at Brian, called him a Maggie bastard, and nutted the one-handed victim in the face, thus providing him with a broken nose to add to his broken hand. All hell broke loose, as there were some NUFC scattered in the vehicle. Even more hell nearly broke loose, as SAFC Kev and some of his wild mates later had to be dissuaded by Brian not to seek out that brave bloke.

After that, and the first leg draw, Brian was fit enough to join the rest at St James and it was another 2-2 draw, this time with another ex-

Blyth player, Alan Shoulder, getting one of the goals. Then came the penalty shoot-out. Anyone who knows Newcastle United and penalty shoot-outs will immediately guess the outcome. The Evening Chronicle did a piece years later listing the history of success, or lack of it, on such occasions, and had to fish out some triumph against Stanley or Consett or somebody in some Cup-tie in ancient history in an attempt to balance up a catalogue of disasters. Sunderland went through, and Brian went home, with a broken hand, a broken nose, and a broken heart – all courtesy of his team.

Generally, this era was a very dour, miserable period in the Black & White lives of the Mag tribe. Home games were seen as something to do on a Saturday, and the pre-match drinking bouts were the main source of pleasure. If the pub licensing laws had been changed in those days, few of the group would have made it to many of the matches. Venues were important, including the Hofbrauhaus, where strippers entertained until just after 3.00pm. This led either to many being late for the game, or, in the case of Benji and a couple of the other Shiney lads, just staying to the bitter, or rather entertaining, end, and getting a bus back home instead.

One match was not exactly dour, but was exceptionally miserable. In February 1979 the old enemy arrived at St James, and Sunderland left with a 4-1 victory, with the help of a Gary Rowell hat-trick. This did not exactly make life easy back in the village. Few players bring any happy memories of those days, and clearly Gary Rowell is not one of them. Peter Withe was one who did, as the centre forward tried to carry on the United Number 9 tradition with pride. To some extent he did so, despite the lack of quality surrounding him. With's signing is also remembered as one of those rare decisions made by Bill McGarry – a successful one.

Also in 1980, there was still no sign of any real promotion push, but one notorious fixture has to be mentioned: the visit of West Ham to Newcastle. The result was a 0-0 draw, but the result off the pitch was far more dramatic and serious. Word had reached Tyneside that the Hammers hooligan hard core were coming up to take the town and give the Geordies hell. Few realise there was also some political element involved, as many of them were allegedly National Front. The impact of news of this impending visit led to the emergence of some pretty wild locals in town, some joining the wild locals already ensconced in half of the now open Leazes End, which was home to those who liked to be next to away fans. On this occasion, Brian and Bobby (and quite a few others) left their normal spot in the Corner, and entered the Leazes.

Bobby himself was a very interesting character. Shot by the Provisional IRA on a deserted West Belfast street, he left the army. Later in life, a devoted left-winger, he was arrested on a Miners' picket line. Later still, he was a nurse in Bensham.

Nursing was definitely not on the agenda as the Cockney skinheads tried to shelter from deluges of stones, bricks, and snooker balls raining down upon them from one half of the

Leazes and from the East Stand corner. Some overshot, and thus Newcastle fans managed to hit Newcastle fans. The worst moment came in the shape of a petrol bomb, which fortunately did not inflict too much damage on the Hammers, although one or two were taken to hospital. One of their mothers later said in the Sun that her son was harmless, and just liked a good ruck wherever he went. The behaviour of the Mags fans was not, and cannot be condoned, but most of them had arrived in Newcastle looking for trouble. The song says it all: *He's Only A Poor Little Hammer, His Clothes Are All Tattered And Torn, He Came For A Fight, We Set Him Alight, And Now He Won't Come Anymore.* The areas near the ground were later spray-painted with slogans such as Free the Bomber.

The 1980-81 season opened up with a 2-0 defeat at Sheffield Wednesday, and yet more trouble, this time involving the Mags and the South Yorkshire constabulary. Far more important things were happening than fights with police down there, and Brian got one of his best birthday presents for some time. He and others rejoiced as Bill McGarry was finally sacked, and Arthur Cox arrived as the new manager. In his early days Cox did not set the world alight, and he was not always popular with the fans. Simmering anger was still around against the Board, and a power struggle was under way with the stalwart, dedicated Malcolm Dix trying to take on those who had exploited the fans and lacked any vision except that of taking money out of the punters. Arthur's earlier lack of success led to the famous Gallowgate chant of "Cox Out, Dix In."

Movement came. Cox stayed, thankfully. Dix did not get in, but by March 1981, Lord Bloody Westwood from the hated Board was out. The old Leazes Enders had finally got their wish. So had one of the group, who shall remain nameless, except to say that it was not Brian. On one occasion, on a summer's afternoon, the unnamed one was nearly arrested at York railway station. He spotted the beloved Chairman and started singing *Westwood is A Pirate*. The police intervened, and he reluctantly walked away.

Westwood though was now gone, although much to the irritation of some Mags, somehow emerged later as chairman of the Football League Management Committee. Rutherford left too, a man who had shocked Geordie, Brian, and thousands of others when he had taken on a major role only to indicate that his real passion was for rugby and not soccer. Stan Seymour was now at the helm.

In the month before this, the FA Cup played one of its usual tricks, providing a home tie against Exeter City in front of 36,000 fans. Amazingly, a Cup run was underway, and this was a fifth round tie. United held the mighty Exeter to a 1-1 draw, and then travelled to the other St James Park, managing to get beat 4-0. All were gutted, but Brian did not get down there, which ensured that his pain and anger did not compare to that felt at Wrexham back in 1978. That scar was too deep, and would only face competition after a Carling Cup match at Wigan in the long distant future.

Chapter Fourteen

Happy Birthday from Mr Keegan

Arthur Cox was desperately trying to rebuild United, but seemed to be making no major impact. The 1981-82 season saw them finish ninth, with only one particularly bright spot on the horizon in the form of Imre Varadi. Then, suddenly and stunningly, as is often the case in the history of Newcastle United, life dramatically changed for the better. The day before yet another birthday, Kevin Keegan stepped out onto the pitch wearing a Black & White strip. Who wanted Cox Out now? The Black & White half of the region went berserk, and bedlam broke out as fans tried to get into the ground to see Keegan's debut. The noise was at exceptionally high decibel levels.

Keegan later said that the Gallowgate sucked his inevitable goal into that net. Many of the characters were there, Bobby, brother Dave, and so on, and if later claims are to be believed, there must have been 300,000 in the ground.

Only Gus, "fresh" from his stag night the night before, failed to get into the ground. He did try to climb over a wall, but a combination of a very bad hangover and the presence of the coppers, with the threat of sleeping off his bad head in the cells, persuaded him to come down. One very special person did get in, although the group, and the rest of the tribe, did not know him.

They would all learn to know him only too well. It was young Alan Shearer from Gosforth, queuing up to see his hero.

It was Keegan's day. Any memories of his destruction of United in the 1974 Cup Final were instantly erased, in true Soviet Union style, and he was now a Geordie. Curiously enough, he was a kind of Geordie anyway. His grandfather had been a hero in the Stanley Pit Disaster, and his Dad, like so many others from the North East, had taken his young family south – to Yorkshire – looking for work. Anyway, Keegan's first goal was enough to see QPR defeated 1-0. The big club was back in town, well, on the way to being on the way to being back in town. Another new dawn, and it would lead them all to their rightful place in the top league of English football.

King Kev's appearance coincided in a new phase in Brian's life. He was now in the middle of writing a PhD on the Spanish Civil War – later unsubmitted, hence no Doctor Brian. During part of the climb into Division 1, his research took him to London. He shared accommodation with Dougie, a Perth St Johnstone fan. Perth is the venue for the Sainties, as should be stressed when discussing that club A vanload of Sunderland fans once visited Johnstone for a pre-season friendly, failing to understand that that town is a very long way from Perth. Unlike those Mackems, Dougie knew where his home team played. He would also visit St. James in the years to come.

The other character in this accommodation set-up was Bedlington Stan. Brian and the Jock disagreed with Bedlington

Stan's Thatcherite politics, and Bedlington Stan and Brian disagreed with the Jock about Newcastle United. They spent endless amounts of energy trying to convince him that NUFC were the biggest club in England and had the most fanatical supporters, but to no avail. Dougie remains unconvinced about the biggest club in England claim to this day, but now agrees about the description of the fans. Still, they had some good football crack, and the social life was lively, and pretty safe too, as the Northumberland member of the trio had a black belt in karate and could handle himself if it was needed. His Geordie macho image was slightly tarnished when his girlfriend came down and said they were off to the ballet, as Stan was a big ballet fan. He'd kept that quiet.

Life in London was a laugh, although all three felt like foreigners, as most Southerners seemed to regard them as from another country. One actually was a foreigner, whilst the other two, technically at least, were not. Brian was interested in a foreigner from another continent, Susanna from Bogota in Columbia, where a certain Tino Asprilla would grow up before joining United in the 1990s. His cup final with Susanna took place in her flat in West London, only for Brian to miss an open goal. He'd forgot to get the blobs, or contraceptives as they are known in the medical world. The moment was lost, and she was soon hanging around with some bearded leftie South American lecturer, preferring him to the exceptionally sophisticated and intellectual United fan - another love lost.

But Brian's main love was not deserting

him. When in London, he managed to get to away games in the South, and also took in Leeds away, which as usual, meant high adrenalin levels and even higher tensions in that town. Back from London, home games were attended, as Cox began to build a side ready to challenge for promotion under Keegan's direction.

Chapter Fifteen

Promotion in Luxembourg

In the summer of 1983, just as United were about to embark upon the big push into the big time, Brian decided to leave the country and live in Luxembourg. Struggling to complete his PhD, having been told to rewrite a couple of chapters, he was offered a job as a researcher with the Socialist Group in the European Parliament. It was a temporary contract for a year, with the prospect of a permanent post. After a few seconds of consideration – the money was fantastic – the PhD went into the attic, and by September Brian was living in a flat with Horst the German and Carlos the Spaniard.

It was a new world, although football talk was thin on the ground, as only Anna, a Florence supporter, and Karin, an Odense supporter from Denmark, really liked the game. Anna became a good friend, and still keeps a NUFC scarf in her wardrobe, whilst Karin became an even better one in a different and more physical way. There was later talk of the pair living as pig farmers in Denmark, but this did not materialise.

Life was interesting and exciting, and involved listening to Edith Piaf songs in cafes, and regular travel to Brussels and Strasbourg. One fiasco in the latter town led to Brian accidentally visiting a brothel, mistaking it for a bar. Naturally, he decided not to leave before finishing his pint.

After several approaches from the girls, he agreed to buy one a drink, and had a brief chat with her. It cost him an absolute fortune, but after an initial refusal to pay, one look at the two hefty bouncers saw the bill settled. He was carrying half of his wages, and instantly knew that he would not only lose some of his looks, but also all his money as well. Foolishly, he told Carlos about the incident, who then told everybody at work, missing out the fact that Brian had not stayed in that bloody brothel.

All this was a long way from Gallowgate, and there was no modern-day communication system which allowed exiles to watch the Mags on tv or use their mobiles or computers. The Pink and telephone calls for information were the only source of keeping up to date. The football paper took on its familiar role again, landing in the post during the week via Mam. Like a good son, Brian telephoned his Mam every Saturday night - for a results update. Karin seemed offended that he would rush out of the flat, even if imminent passion was on the cards, to get down to the phones at the railway station, but she gradually adapted to this behaviour. More detailed calls to brother Dave often occurred, naturally from the office.

On one occasion, a couple of Danes were on the deck with laughter as Brian spoke to brother Dave about United in his natural dialect. When the phone was put down, he angrily asked why they were laughing at him, and they quickly explained that it was because he had sounded like he was speaking West Danish, yet in a foreign language.

There were no games to watch, apart from a visit from Ingerland, and Brian was not interested in that anyway. Their hooligans spent a couple of days smashing up Luxembourg City, and terrorising old grannies, and a group of Cockneys visited the local British-style pub of Horst, Carlos, and Brian. They immediately shouted racist abuse at the black Portuguese barmaid, Nena, and Horst, a gentle giant measuring 6ft 7in, with hands like shovels, asked them to apologise. The leader expressed glee that they had found a Kraut, and then expressed horror when the slumped Horst stood up, warning him that he, and at least four of his twenty-strong gang would be put out of the window unless they left. This they did, and Brian warned Horst that they had to leave too, as that group would be bound to return in greater numbers. Nena was already arranging protection.

One weekend there was a visit from a group of Shiney tourists. True to form, after a couple of pints Mogga burst into NUFC songs. He was accompanied by Sam, Den, and Lofty. Brian did manage to obtain some detailed information on events at St James, but not on the first night. They arrived late, and hardly said a word as they emptied his fridge of the food which was supposed to last until Sunday night. A foolish offer of a sightseeing tour on the Saturday morning was rejected in favour of just looking at a view from a cafe bar. The rest of the weekend remains a blur, as does the Monday morning in Brussels when Brian was supposed to be taking notes in a meeting.

The days in Luxembourg eventually

ended, but not without Brian acting as a Second
Best Man for Horst. This was a tradition in part of
southern Germany, and he was forced to pretend
that he could speak German. His stress was only
relieved by the fact that the wedding do was held
in a village called Scheit – pronounced Shite – so
he bought a set of postcards, a very rare event,
and sent them back to the Shiney Mags. Karin was
with him in that June, but soon she had to return
to Denmark, and he had to return to the North
East. So, no career in pig-farming then.

Brian had managed to get back home on
occasions during his Luxembourg exile. The visit
at Christmas confirmed that this exciting side was
really on the rise. The only dampener on that
break involved Lyn, NUFC, partner of Min, SAFC,
organising a party for a televised FA Cup match
on a Friday night. Lyn was the woman who easily
won the argument about their baby daughter's
religious upbringing – it was Black & White, much
to Min's discontent. That FA Cup party, with an
eager gathering including Mogga, the singer, and
Sam, the man who had to be knocked out of bed
for home games, was a total disaster. All seemed
to dismiss the fact that the opposition was
Liverpool – shades of 1974 – and the game was at
Anfield. Millions watched a 4-0 hammering, which
later led Keegan to conclude he could not play in
Division 1 and had to retire.

Recovery came quickly however, and
another return on work leave, this time in the
Easter, saw Carlisle hammered 5-1, with Mogga
and the rest rolling around the Gallowgate, as
Beardsley and Keegan notched two each, and
Waddle got the other. Brian was back in his

Luxembourg flat as some of his mates, including brother Dave, spent a mad night in Huddersfield, celebrating promotion. This was a fantastic time, glorious days, and once again, a period when it made it all worthwhile for so many thousands.

United were back in the Big Time.

Chapter Sixteen

A year with Maggie

On that Easter return for Carlisle at home, there was only one dark cloud on the horizon, and it had nothing to do with the club. The early 80s had seen the full force of Margaret Thatcher's policies, and thousands had been thrown on the dole. It was now time for her biggest challenge. Brian sat at the back of the local miners' hall to hear defiant pledges to face up to her and save the pits. This was a match that the miners would not win. In fact, it was no match at all, as that bastard woman used the power of her state to crush the striking miners. They held out for a year and there was terrible hardship and pain for so many Mags, and Sunderland fans too, across the region. Brother Dave, the other Brian and another Brian, Micky and Paul – Fr Steve's brothers – Jackie, and another Kevin, were all directly affected.

Football talk did not stop, and often provided some relief, but this was a rare period when it was not always top of the agenda. Brian was partly involved in this confrontation with Thatcher, trying to support brother Dave and some of his mates, and helping out with some food parcel collections. In the autumn, Dad, who had predicted the defeat, passed away. At least Dad's own inner turmoil was over, albeit against a background of a community up against the wall.

Buses full of coppers would pass through the village, with their inhabitants waving £10 notes at the villagers, and by March 1985, they all trooped back to the pits, broken and defeated by That Evil Woman and her cohorts.

Life, and NUFC life, had to go on, as always. Whilst some miners sunbathed in the summer of the strike, politics broke out once again inside Gallowgate. Freshly promoted, Arthur Cox walked, insulted by his new contract offer. Keegan had gone as well. In came Big Jack Charlton, the down-to-earth Newcastle fan, unlike his Manc brother Bobby. Jack had a reputation for producing efficient but dull sides, but he inherited a couple of players with tremendous flair in the shape of Beardsley and Waddle.

New Year's Day was certainly not dull, and was an exhilarating one for Sam, Mogga, Lyn, Brian, and the rest. By now Geordie was missing, having emigrated to West Denton. Lyn, caring as ever, felt they had to find Sam before setting off for the local derby. After a heated discussion at her house, he emerged from behind the settee to tell them all to keep the noise down. Sam having been found, the group called into one of the locals for a quick pint and taunt at the SAFC before heading off to watch United destroy their local rivals 3-1 with the help of the little genius Beardsley.

New Year's Eve had already seen the football tension take over some of the strike tension, and the derby dominated most of the crack until dawn. New Year's night saw Mogga singing his head off in a local bar, and most of the crowd trying to have conversations with the local

SAFC. Curiously, they did not seem to want to discuss the game. Yet another Brian, a devoted ex-Fulwell-Ender, did join in a snowball fight with gusto. He had a special reason for disliking his Mag neighbours. His son, influenced by them, was a Mag, much to the yet another Brian's horror.

That was the high point, the Sunderland match that is, not the snowball fight. But as the season ended with a mid-table position, events were about to hit the fans dramatically. In came the era of selling off the family jewels, just like Thatcher was doing in her privatisation programme. Newcastle became the Selling Club big-time, and the trio sold were all very gifted Geordies at that. In the summer, Waddle took off for Spurs. Jack Charlton took off too, after a friendly in the same summer.

Waddle came back with Spurs in March 1986, and scored, naturally, in the 2-2 draw. He received the traditional Geordie welcome for those perceived to have abandoned the club, even though there were guilty parties in the Boardroom, of course. The Gallowgate End bayed, and subjected him to a torrent of abuse, whilst the Corner added a few missiles to the verbal barrage.

An 8-1 defeat at West Ham in April deserves a mention, only if for the fact that the team lost their two goalies. Peter Beardsley was hopeless – as a goalkeeper, that is.

The summer saw the interlude of another England World Cup, and witnessed some very heated rows between Mogga, Brian, and Sam, against Den and Lofty. The latter pair were not

Mags, but were very much into Ingerland, unlike the other three. The row focused upon the fact that a certain Bobby Robson, already disliked because he dropped Kevin Keegan back in 1982, did not seem to regard Peter Beardsley as an obvious first team choice. Mogga particularly became agitated, not because he was an England fan, but because he rightly knew that this man deserved to be on the world stage. An injury allowed Peter into the team, he teamed up with Gary Lineker, and the rest is history. Although England did not win the World Cup, the two players went on to form a lethal partnership.

The summer of 1987 was not a dull one either at St James. Family Jewel Number 2 was sold, and this time it was Peter. This provoked utter depression amongst many United fans, not least Mogga, who had always been willing to discuss his skills for hours on end, even if nobody was listening to him. The Red Scousers gleefully bought Beardsley when the club refused to offer him a better deal, and he departed amidst correct accusations about them lacking ambition and professionalism. The fans knew he was right, and it somehow seemed different to the Waddle departure. All were gutted and very angry, but the lid was partly taken off the boiling pan by the arrival of the Man from Brazil: *His Name Is Mirandinha, He's Not From Argentina, He's From Brazil, He's Fucking Brill*. The place went Brazil mad. Even Shiney Row had a connection, as Vic, a local lad of Portuguese origin, did some of the interpretation work for Mira before Gazza took over.

At the end of January 1988, the FA Cup

was in town, and brought with it five wonderful goals and a distinct lack of preparation from the club, as usual. They failed to prepare for a larger than normal crowd, even though everybody knew that the Cup always brought the fans back in some hope for some thing. Given that it was not all-ticket, Brian went up to the Gallowgate End earlier than normal, only to see chaotic scenes. He soon found himself crammed against a wall, and decided that it was time to get out and pass the police horses on the way. He feigned injury, was lifted over the crowd, and made his way around to the Paddock. He carried on with his acting role, limping alongside a long, snaking queue. Kick-off was imminent, and two big lads took pity on him – they had seen the chaos around the corner – and pulled him into the front of the queue.

Brian remains grateful to those lads, as Gazza and the rest were brilliant, hammering Swindon. It was a very good day at the office, and later allegations of a betting scandal involving the opposition fail to dampen the wonderful memory of that performance.

The next month was not a good one. Gazza scored again, in the league match against Norwich, United going down 3-1 at home. Brian was living with Jane in Jesmond, and supposed to attend the dinner party she was arranging. Dinner parties were not, and are still not, his normal scene, and on that night they were definitely not on his agenda. He popped into the Cradlewell, had a quick pint – alone – returned to the house, and muttered that he was never gannin' back, and that he was gannin' to bed. He did. This hardly contributed to a harmonious weekend, but when he awoke on the Sunday, he still had that strong feeling that he had had enough. They were sending him to bed in depression.

Jane makes mistake of organizing dinner party on match day

Chapter Seventeen

Moving around & going down

During these years, Brian's life had again taken him to London and back again. In 1985, he worked with the local MP, Roland Boyes, a brilliant bloke dedicated to helping the people of the area. He also tended to mock the Mags, as he preferred Hartlepool, and was occasionally seen at Sunderland, but this did not undermine Brian's admiration for him. By the late summer of 1986, Brian was offered a job in the House of Commons, which again allowed away games in the South, but by the February of 1987, he was sacked or resigned, depending on how the situation is viewed. His Welsh MP employer had a rather bad record with staff, with about nine employees in two years or so - but Brian foolishly thought he could handle that.

On one Friday morning, Brian told the MP that he was going home for a match and was taking the Clipper out of London at 3.00pm to avoid the traffic. This was the old Clipper bus which took Geordies out of London in a good mood, and brought them back on a Sunday night in a bad mood, as most would have preferred working in Newcastle to life in that foreign capital. He was told to expect a phone call from Cardiff at 5.00pm, and to be back at his desk in the Mother of Parliaments. He pointed out that he had worked about sixty hours already that week, and jumped on the Geordie Clipper as planned.

As usual, it was full of ex-pats, smuggling their bottles onto the bus disguised as orange juice, and NUFC was often a major topic of conversation. Back home, and after that match in February, he had a chat with Jane, by now a major player in his life, in a Jesmond flat. Brian wrote out his resignation note on the Sunday night after he had decided not to return on the said Clipper. The next day, the postman was prompt and very kind, as he delivered a letter from the so-called Socialist MP telling Brian that he was sacked, but offering him a pay-off. He naturally threw his resignation letter in the bin, took the money, and ignored the conditions attached to the termination of the job.

Brian's life again changed dramatically, and brought him into contact with another set of Mags. He ended up working in a care home in Shieldfield, and met up with more members of the Black & White tribe. It involved working with the physically disabled elderly, and the Elderly Mentally Infirm. He loved that job. It needed three essential qualities – caring feelings, humour, and mild insanity, amongst the staff that is. Some of the residents loved to talk about their days in the past with United. Many of the staff loved to talk about their days with United in the present.

He met Rob the Chef, an old Leazes-Ender, Tracey from Walker, and above all Scotty. He was passionate about his work with the elderly, passionate about women, and extremely passionate about NUFC. Scotty quickly became a soulmate, partly because of a shared sense of humour, and mainly because of their common bond as dedicated Mags. Within a short spell, Brian and Jane undertook a trial separation, and he was soon sharing a flat with Scotty.

Libel laws do not allow much reference to events at that residence near the Vale in Jesmond, but suffice to say that the Odd Couple Mags were often keen to vacate it, and go up to the Cradlewell to avoid the pressure of care work, or rather avoid telephone calls and knocks on the door from girlfriends. These were stressful times on that front, not helped by the potential threat of a very jealous ex-boyfriend who turned out to be not just fierce but allegedly the owner of a shotgun. Fortunately, he never appeared and neither did his shotgun.

There was also one passionate moment in the flat, when Brian really displayed his inability to understand the opposite sex. After some particularly adventurous time on the floor with a woman who was very special to him, he put on an Irish World Cup game and witnessed them triumph. He stated that this was the highlight of his evening, and this comment did not seem to be appreciated by the female companion, who was not into Ireland or football for that matter.

Normally, the Odd Couple themselves were often absent from the flat on evenings, however, and would return late at night to argue whether Newcastle were the biggest club in the world, or the worst, who was the best or worst signing ever, and often who loved or hated United the most. Sadly, or perhaps fortunately, there are no taped recordings of the Flat tapes on NUFC debates. Their business idea of establishing a Mag counselling centre in a hut behind the Strawberry never progressed, although probably remains a good proposition to this day.

Doctor to Nurse: "I see they've lost again!"

Work in the Shieldfield care home introduced Brian to some brilliant NUFC crack with yet another set of Mags. Rob the Chef no longer attended many games, but it did not make him less of a fan. He had done his time, and still studied the fortunes of the club with intensity and considerable knowledge. Like so many others, Norah had a son whose life seemed to revolve around United. Nancy, the boss, regarded devotion to the club as perfectly natural. Ella, mother of Scotty, who as well as bringing much-needed food to the flat from Hebburn, always tried to sound optimistic about the fate of the team. At least Ella tried. By this stage Brian's Mam tended to predict that NUFC would never win a thing. By the late 80s she had given up trying to boost the morale of her sons and the others.

Other characters emerged. Big Mark came to work at the care home. He was a Durham lad who followed Newcastle. Big Mark had a strong dislike for Bill McGarry, not least because the old disciplinarian had told him to leave the youth squad at St James because he ate too much. His partner Debbie, a Benwell lass, was also Black & White daft, although she never attended games.

There was also a good friend of Scotty's from Walker. He didn't work with the group, but was a good footballer, and was therefore put into the staff seven-a-side team as a useful ringer. His name was Mick, later known as Mad Mick and future DJ at Idols in Newcastle. Mick is now part-owner of the Back Page in town, so much better than the official NUFC shop. Whilst Mick's shop is successful, his career with the seven-a-side team

"Must be a big game – Micky's turned up"

was not. It has to be said that his appearances
were erratic, or rather he never turned up much.

For some inexplicable reason, Mad Mick
was involved in arranging a bizzare trip to watch
some play-off between Boro and Bradford City.
Brian, Big Mark, and Scotty accompanied him. It
was a freebie of some kind, and took them into
the seats. Mick berated a Boro fan for not singing,
telling him it was an important match. They then
found themselves amongst the elite after the
match, helping themselves to free food and drink.

Then came the 1988-89 season. The
summer was not dull. As usual The Selling Club
were at it again, and this time it was the incredibly
talented young Geordie from Dunston, Gazza,
leaving for Chris Waddle's Tottenham Hotspur. It
was uproar time again. Brian returned from a
Spanish holiday with Jane, an increasingly
important figure in his life again, and opened the
flat door. Scotty gave him a detailed run-down on
events. McFaul had used the money to buy the
big and useful Wimbledon goalkeeper, Dave
Beasant, John Hendrie, John Robertson, and a
centre half, Andy Thorn. Scotty sang the praises of
Thorn. He soon confirmed that he did not really
know much about Thorn, but added he was
brilliant anyway. Brian believed his flatmate, and
despite the loss of Gazza, pre-season optimism
took over, with the latter now regarded as a
traitor. It was birthday time again, and United
went down 4-0 at Everton. They also went down
into Division 2 - relegation time again.

The fixture list that season was
particularly unkind to Gazza, as he had to return
in early September with his mate Waddle, and the

fashionable Cockneys. A sudden urge to buy Mars
Bars swept the area, and some of the group were
spotted queuing up to buy them – none of them
had previously been seen buying chocolate
before a match. They were, of course, presents for
the Dunston boy, who had admitted his liking for
them, and Brian spent half the match in the
Corner trying to avoid Mars Bars, and other
objects, hitting him on the head as they rained
down toward the player every time he
approached that area of the ground. Unlike
Waddle, who naturally scored in the 2-2 draw,
Gazza was unable to handle the antagonism and
hatred. He was finally put out of his agony,
substituted to a background of foul-mouthed
abuse, much to his obvious distress. He should

"No Mars Bars – Gazza's bought the lot!"

have understood that, whatever the reasons, leaving the Mags was seen as betrayal.

By November, the relegation bandwagon was well and truly on its way. The 4-0 away defeat at Millwall confirmed it, and saw some NUFC trying to attack the Board, and not the locals, much to the total bemusement of the latter. Brian was not there on that day, but he did visit the Den on other occasions. It was, as they say, a very difficult place to go to, and not for football reasons. One fixture saw part of the London Underground lines cut off, as the two sets of fans clashed. Another saw a group leave Newcastle with the aim of meeting Harry the Dog, one of the Millwall leaders, as he had previously appeared on television boasting about his hooligan reputation. They met him inside the Den, and Harry was not happy.

Fr Steve too once visited Millwall. He managed to find a bar full of their hardcore, and emerged an hour later accompanied by the brother-in law of the landlord. Fr Steve had entered the bar, and, much to the horror of his brothers Paul and Mick, loudly ordered the beers in his Durham accent. The evil-looking characters twitched, ready for action, and the suspicious bar owner asked him where he was from. Fr Steve said Newcastle, but added he lived just over the river in Hackney. The suspicious one asked him where, and although his priestly profession was not revealed, he confirmed that it was at the famous St Joseph's hospice. The landlord welcomed him and the brothers with open arms, and called off the Dogs of War in the corner. He had a tin to collect money for the hospice, and knew of some of the caring work which took place over there. He later ordered his brother-in-law to take the group down to the ground, and make sure that they joined their Geordie comrades safely.

By the end of the season United were down and very much out. A paltry crowd attended the last home match, part of a protest against those in power who had brought the club to this dire level - again. A local vicar was filmed on BBC saying a prayer for the future of the club. It certainly did need some help from the Big Man.

Divine intervention needed - Vicar prays for the Mags

Chapter Eighteen

Boycotts & Bloody Play-offs!

Whilst United were on the move down, Brian was on the move as well. "Ower the watta", as Scotty would say. It was over the Tyne into the Avenues in Bensham, or Saltwell as some prefer to call it. Shortly after that 4-0 defeat at Everton, Brian left Scotty behind and moved into an old terraced house over the other side of the Tyne, with Jane. As that eventful season kicked off, his own life did as well. In the August he was offered a job as a political researcher with the dedicated and hard-working Gateshead MP, Joyce Quin, at a salary double that of his one in the Shieldfield Residential Home. Even so, Brian needed a fortnight to consider it before accepting the post. Leaving that job was a wrench, and not just because of the daily NUFC football chats with Rob, Scotty, and just about anybody else passing through.

The leaving day itself was difficult, mainly due to the fact that Nancy and the staff had arranged for a so-called social worker to visit the party inside the home, only the social worker was a stripagram. Brian was humiliated in front of his scheming colleagues, and the cheering residents. It was later rumoured that a couple of the older men had to go to bed afterwards, due to heart strain.

In September 1989 Brian and Jane were

married by, who else but Fr Steve. The following March, on the first day of Spring, a wonderful, lovely, precious new Mag emerged at the Queen Elizabeth hospital: baby daughter Claire, another NUFC addition. By the time she was a toddler, she was aware that United were important in her Dad's life. Brian trained her not to disturb him for ten minutes as he read the back page of the Journal on early Saturday mornings. Work-wise, Brian did his research, and soon gained a reputation in the office for being fully up to speed with his knowledge of latest developments in the press early on Monday mornings - on Mag-related events that is. The politics had to wait.

Life in the Avenues and in Gateshead politics was generally good, and it naturally brought him into contact with new United fanatics, some of whom are still very much still on the current scene. The Azure Blue was the local, ran by the famous Tyneside bar owner, Viv. He was not actually a football fan, but was an incredible character. He was a hard man – he had to be, as he was gay, not easy when he used to run rough pubs in the 1960s. He was a caring man too, making sure that some of his rough-looking regulars left their pints and took up dinners for some of the old-timers who could no longer make it to the bar. He called Brian a sheep-shagger – something to do with being from Shiney – but he ran a good bar. The lads in his hostelry, unlike Viv, did talk NUFC.

The local political crowd and councillors were dedicated fans too. Norman and Joe, with their respective offspring, Steve and Big Shaun. Steve was always brilliant for crack on the local

bus as he made his way to the Ministry in
Longbenton, and Big Shaun would, as the decade
moved on, appear in Joe's seat next to Brian.
Curiously, he could be potentially wild if he was
out in Gateshead High Street, but was totally calm
and studious at matches themselves. Perhaps he
was just that type of fan, or perhaps he was under
strict orders from his father. There were other
United fans around too, not least Ian, and Bill and
Gordon, who were still bitterly scarred by the
1974 Cup Final and quite cynical towards their
club. Yet another Brian, Peter, and Pat, the
matriach of a very large family of Mags such as
Adam, Nick, and their Uncle Fred.

    Nick had a connection with brother Dave,
and Bryan, another fanatic. They were all
councillors in Sunderland, as Washington was of
in theory part of that town. They never hid their
Mag credentials, always made sure they did not
have to attend any meeting which got in the way
of a match. One vital meeting took place one
Saturday morning in the early 90s. Bryan and
Dave turned up with their Black & White tops,
much to the resentment of some of the other
Sunderland councillors. Bryan and Dave dashed
out of the meeting, landing in Leicester via
Bryan's driving three hours later. He still claims
that brother Dave's knuckles were white, as was
his face, throughout that rather fast journey.

    They also found themselves the recipients
of hate mail when they were involved in planning
decisions for the future Stadium of Light. They
faced difficulties if forced to attend a gathering
involving Sunderland FC. On one of its rare
successful moments, brother Dave stayed five

minutes at some reception for their players, told one of them that he was a Mag when he was in the toilet, and just left. Brother Dave had his principles.

In August 1989 United were back in Division 2, also back were the big-time protests against the hated Board. Over the years, many fans had made their individual protests against the people exploiting them, but on this occasion, a more extremist element of the Anti-Board campaign called for a Boycott. Brian joined the extremists, naturally, and watched United in the packed Cannon pub in Low Fell, on a video showing the 1974 semi-final triumph against Burnley, with those Supermac goals looking as great as ever. Similar scenes took place across the region.

It later turned out that Bryan, the Washington councillor, was over at St James trying to persuade fans not to go into the home game as it would mark support for the Board, and not the team. He was a key player in the United Supporters for Change movement, and had also taken a lead role in gaining permission for pubs to show that FA Cup semi. Brian was in the company of Ian, one of the local politicians, and this was the day they cemented a NUFC bond which is still seen in the Irish Centre on match days. Ian was, and is, a larger-than-life character, famous less for his relatively successful political career, more for his whistling at matches. Anybody who has stood within ten yards of him will know him, or will certainly have heard him.

While Supermac was scoring against Burnley in the Cannon that day, a new standard-bearer of the Number 9 shirt, and a good one at that, Micky Quinn, banged in four goals at Gallowgate against Leeds, the old enemy. Boycott or no boycott, Ian and Brian trooped off to Monie's paper shop to get the Pink. Some could not maintain the protest for long, and soon felt the withdrawal from the Black & White drug just too hard to endure. By the end of September, Brian was in the Clock Stand at Roker Park, so at least he felt he was still part of the organised stay-away from Gallowgate. The Shiney Mags had tickets for the United end, and he cut a lonely figure sitting amongst a group of Sunderland hardcore hooligans. He pretended to be the boring lad, disinterested in football, who somehow had just come along for the game, but blew his unconvincing cover quickly when he failed to jump up when they got their first corner.

One of their leaders, who had already been in a major confrontation with some Mags who had landed earlier and had been led off into the Roker End, was sitting next to him. He did not believe Brian was the boring lad disinterested in football. The result was 0-0 on the pitch, and a huge amount of cigarettes off it. The leader leaned over the stray United fan, telling him that if he supplied regular tabs, he would not inform his wild companions that they had an unwanted visitor amongst them. He was subsequently well supplied. Half-time was difficult as it involved serious thought on whether to return to that seat. Brian did so, but he was not over-trusting this bloke though, and left a few minutes before the end, moving rapidly out of that stadium.

One famous match stood out on New

Year's Day 1990, mainly because of brother Dave's prediction to Mogga, Sam, and the rest, that the Wolves centre forward, Steve Bull, was totally useless and any talk of him playing for England was ridiculous. They all nodded enthusiastically, or rather nodded, as it was New Year's Day, and they had been up until 7.00am in the morning. Brother Dave has spent the rest of his life avoiding any optimistic predictions about NUFC and taking any sign of success with extreme caution. By half time Steve Bloody Bull had scored a hat-trick, and Wolves won 4-1. Brother Dave of course is far from alone in making disastrous predictions. Very few United fans have not been caught out in some of their ill-fated statements or assessments about matches or the future of certain players.

After Bull, February witnessed a Cup run, leading to a fifth round tie at home to Manchester United, although few felt Wembley was in sight this time. Dougie, the Perth St Johnstone fan, came down. He managed to be sick in the fireplace the night before, and saw a decent effort against the Mancs, but a defeat. This was no big deal, as the push for promotion was under way. It led all the way to a play-off, taking in a Boro away match on a giant screen at St James which confirmed that automatic promotion was not on the cards as the Smoggies put four goals in. Scotty and Brian attended the game, at Gallowgate that is, as away tickets were like gold-dust.

Pre-SKY and all those mobiles, United had attempted to enter the early stages of the modern communication age, charging the fans a fair amount of money for the pleasure. The giant screen was totally blurred, and it had nothing to do with the Teesside chemical plants. It was a total cock-up as fans ignored the tannoy announcer asking them not to invade the pitch, and got as close as they could to the blur. They could just make out that it was play-off time - against Sunderland.

The ex-flatmates met in one of their old familiar haunts, the Cradlewell in Jesmond, as Jim Smith, the Bald Eagle, prepared his side to finish off the SAFC after a useful draw in the first leg. The two were no friends of Smith, as they instinctively felt he had no real passion for the club. They were right, as years later, he confirmed that he never really enjoyed life up here, and complained that too many fans wanted to pick the team. He had missed the point of course – he should have been pleased that he was at a place where thousands of thousands of people wanted to pick the team. That night in the Cradlewell was neither the time nor the place to complain about Jim Smith, and there was no mention of him. Indeed, for a long spell, there was no mention of anything connected with the club, including the game. It was unknown for those two, and anxiety had clearly taken on new levels.

The pair played pool, talked about life, but did not mention football. It was if they knew something. The silence about the forthcoming game was finally broken when Scotty looked at Brian, and with his steely eyes, suggested that they knew what was going to happen, didn't they? About three hours later, after two Sunderland goals and a pitch invasion, brother Dave and all the rest dejectedly and despairingly left the ground. Bedford Town, Hereford, Liverpool 1974, Wrexham, and other events had all hurt, but this was a pretty huge wound which certainly ranked alongside that hurtful collection. They had let the Mag army down again, when it really, really mattered, losing a chance to get promoted, and worse still, at the hands of their gleeful neighbours from down the road.

Scotty and Brian met up in Fitzgeralds afterwards, bought a pint, and left for Jesmond and Gateshead respectively. Silence dominated again, only this time without any talk at all, let alone about football. Brian crossed the Tyne, swearing that he would not inflict this misery upon his new-born baby Claire, who of course was at St James by the age of six.

Chapter Nineteen

Walking into Wonderland

The 1991-92 season disintegrated into chaos under the new manager, Ossie Ardiles, the former Argentian World Cup star. The fans never hated Ossie as such, as he relied upon a young side on a learning curve, and tried to play exciting football. By January 1992, in a typical game at St James, against Charlton Athletic, his team managed to go 3-1 up by half-time, only to go down 4-3 by full time. The visionary John Hall was now in full control of the Board. Hall, apparently persuaded by his son Douglas and Freddie Fletcher, reluctantly sacked Ossie and appointed a man who had been out of football for years and had never managed a club in his life: Kevin Keegan. It was chaos time again in town, and thus began the Keegan years.

So much has been recorded about the Keegan Revival. It began on a high, with an emphatic home victory against Bristol City in early February, but it was not quite that simple. He brought in Brian - Brian Killer Kilcline – popular with the fans partly because of his nickname, which indicated his approach to any forward, and Sheedy, to boost the left wing. The revival ran into trouble, with Keegan, his assistant Terry McDermott and John Hall desperately trying to avoid the drop into the old Third Division. Some worried that the club may have faced extinction,

but this would never have happened, as the Black
& Whites would have emerged in some form or
other, even if it was on some playground in Byker.
And if they had reached the final of the Northern
Breweries Piss-Up Cup, they would have needed a
bigger stadium to get the fans in.

Still, it was deadly serious business in
those early Keegan months, and fortunately never
led to an appearance at a Byker playground. They
survived, but only just. In late April, brother Dave
sent Brian flying down the Gallowgate End – again
– as David Kelly got the goal against Portsmouth,
later telling him that he would never see a more
important goal in his lifetime. Brother Dave would
often repeat that phrase, and mutter "David Kelly,
David Kelly", to his younger sibling over the years.

The following week saw Brian pacing
around a garden cottage in Harbottle, in a gazebo.
He had never heard of a gazebo – they never had
them in Shiney – but it turned out to be a small
greenhouse-type structure like some kind of Tardis
from Dr Who. It had a radio, which was the most
important thing, and, the Mags survived the drop at
Leicester. Jane had wisely taken baby Claire out for
the afternoon, as Brian prowled around that
gazebo liked a caged animal listening to the radio.
His shouting and jumping around managed to
alarm passing walkers heading for the heights of
the Cheviot Hills. The 2-1 victory ensured that
United were still in Division 2, but only by the skin
of their teeth.

King Kev was now preparing for the
march out of that miserable league, and Norman,
Joe, and Brian had already joined him for that
planned journey a few months before. After an

intense discussion in the Azure Blue in the Avenues, the three were already season ticket holders as the bandwagon rolled out of the Central into the top league. They based their strategy on the basic theory – it had been shit-or-bust time, or sink-or-swim back in that February, and they had taken the risk. They would not regret it, as the Mag tribes crammed into St James into the autumn of 1992, and Mr Keegan took his team into that swimming pool at Olympic pace.

"Ten out of Ten", as the video is known. The season opened with a 3-2 victory against Southend, with Lee Clark, a dedicated Geordie. Clark was one of Scotty's main heroes, as he was from his part of town. And then it exploded, with the ten victories out of ten. This astonishing route back to the Big Time was only temporarily derailed by Grimsby at home, and led to some joy for Paddy, an emigre from Cleethorpes living in the Avenues near Brian. It mattered little for the Mags, as it stopped the SAFC halting the run, and Paddy was quite pleased.

The relentless march was soon restored, not least by O'Brien at Roker Park. Another O'Brien would also score against the Mackems years later, thus leading to the song, *O'Brien, O'Brien, Any Any Any OBrien, Who Put The Ball In The Makem's Net, O'Brien, O'Brien.* The Sunderland fans could only look on in envy in that "Ten Out Of Ten" season as nothing could stand in the way of that high speed Geordie Express. It was simply unstoppable.

Again, games stand out in that season. One was a rare defeat at Barnsley, in early winter, when Joe, Brian, brother Dave, and Big Shaun travelled down to Oakwell, but enjoyed the old standing terrace atmosphere which was allowed in the lower leagues. Mags sought out drinking-holes, in their thousands, and failed to find many, and entered a rather gloomy, grim end. They sang long and loud as always, and the defeat was not too much of a concern. The old friend, the FA Cup turned up just after New Years Day. This was particularly good news for Brian, as he was trapped in the festive clutches of the in-laws in some obscure, dreary part of West London, Maidenhead actually.

Brian managed to escape and got over to Kings Cross station to catch the train up to see the cup tie against Port Vale, who were slain 2-0. Inevitably, he left behind a domestic dispute, as Jane was not too pleased he was off to the match, but he knew that the young Claire, then aged three, oblivious to the tension, would have joined him as her Mag education developed in later years.

In February, Brian met up with Fat Baz, the Blackburn fan from university days who was now in textiles, well, selling ladies' underwear actually, although he did eventually move on to become a factory manager in Casablanca. Brian took the opportunity to boast to an unconvinced Fat Baz that the Mags were on the way back. They saw Jack Straw, a future Home Secretary in the New Labour Government, but paid little attention to him. In fact, Barry paid more attention to the fact that the normal home bar was packed out with Geordies. Nowt new there again. United lost, and despite a brief wait at Preston railway station – not one of his most popular sites after the incident some years before – he caught the train home via

Carlisle and had some good crack with some Haltwhistle and Hexham NUFC. There was slight depression, but far from the clinical sense, as all Mags knew that the top league was just around the corner.

By now, there was a new kid on the Number 9 block, Andy Cole who *Gets the Ball, Scores A Goal, Andy, Andy Cole*. Apart from blasting in goals in the true tradition of that shirt, he certainly achieved something else on Tyneside, by sending most of the minority racist element into hiding. Any criticism of Andy, or worse, of his colour, risked a lynching. He perhaps did more than most to drive away the far right. The Tyne and Wear Anti-Fascist Association (TWAFA) had previously done a tremendous job with their slogans in the 1980s, and with their badges proclaiming that Geordies were Black and White, a far better job than any politician could have done. Even TWAFA however could not compete – and still cannot – with the appearance of a top Mag black footballer, and his impact upon the younger generations.

On 9th May 1993 Andy Cole confirmed that United were back, banging in another hat-trick, along with David Kelly, brother Dave's hero, who also banged in a hat-trick, with General Robert E Lee joining in as well. Leicester were hammered 7-1, and United soared into the Premiership. Brian, meanwhile, nearly soared out of the East Stand, courtesy of Joe, who hugged, pushed, and threw him in the air, on seven occasions. Many others in the capacity 30,000 crowd were no doubt experiencing similar things.

The Mags were back!

Chapter Twenty

Black & White explosion

The Keegan era brought with it an explosion on the Tyneside football-crazy public, and stimulated new levels of intense passion and obsession. This was the beginning of the real age of the strip, still very much alive and kicking, of course, and not just on a match day, as many a visitor to the area has pointed out. Some used to wear versions in the 1980s, but now they were everywhere: at bus stops, on street corners, across the city and the towns, and even in churches. In various parts of the region, it was unwise to leave a strip on the washing line, as it stood every chance of disappearing. Keegan-mania was everywhere.

Sitting in his backyard one night, Brian heard his neighbour Mickey shouting "Keegan, Keegan" for a few minutes. This was not particularly odd, but the voice was becoming louder and more agitated. Brian peered over the wall, to see Mickey training his new puppy dog, Keegan. Monei's newsagent was packed, and people were hanging around outside every Saturday night, waiting for the arrival of the Football Pink. If it was late, they, and particularly Monei the owner, became increasingly agitated. Normally mild-mannered, he would be on the phone either to Thomson House in the town or to fellow angry Indian Geordie newsagents asking if their Pinks had arrived.

Meanwhile, the punters, including Brian and Big Mark, the latter from the residential care work days, would grow increasingly restless. Big Mark had moved in with Debbie, and Mark and Brian would take their Pinks up to the Azure Blue lounge, study the paper in detail as if in a library, and then debate just how far their football club could go. The Pink was a valuable commodity, although its colour did cause confusion one early Monday morning at the bus stop, when one lad asked Brian if he could have a look at it. He was crestfallen when Brian explained he was carrying the Financial Times for work research.

Big Mark and his fellow Pink reader did have one particular claim to fame at a later stage, with their innocent but major role in the infamous boycott of Sugar Puffs in Sunderland. Keegan did the advert, acting as the Honey Monster. Mark told Brian that he had heard a snippet on Radio Newcastle that, as a consequence, some fans in Mackem City were refusing to buy the product. Brian told a contact at the Guardian sports section on the Friday. By Monday morning the story had been picked up by the tabloids, and all hell broke loose.

Mark's wife Debbie, herself a fanatic, acted as hostess for one particular game. It was a derby against Sunderland, scheduled for the dinnertime on police orders. This was a familiar attempt to stop alcohol consumption, but usually failed as some pubs just opened illegally at 8.30am. Mark invited Brian and brother Dave over to his flat for 9.00am in order to consume cans of beer, discuss football, and watch porn on TV before this midday game. Debbie never blinked, and produced some bacon sandwiches. Her brother John is worthy of a mention. He was on the dole, and hardly ever went out, except for a match, where he would spend what little money he had on getting in to see United. As ticket access became more difficult, Mark helped him out, ensuring his brother-in-law could still get into some games.

United entered the age of SKY. Joe provided the sitting room and the beer, and Jenny laid out the sandwiches for Norman, Ian, Big Shaun and Brian to watch away matches. The games had already become ticket-only back in the promotion push, and as time passed the ground became season-ticket only. Sadly, many fanatical Mags, including brother Dave, were pushed aside, unable to meet the cost of entry for a full season up front. Many others begged, borrowed, or perhaps even stole, to obtain the money. The ground was too small, and season tickets were very valuable items indeed. It was not uncommon to hear conversations about somebody's holiday plans, illness, or something even worse, only for an instant enquiry as to the whereabouts of their ticket. Giant Toon flags passed around the ground, but sadly were banned in later years.

The driving force behind this Black & White revolution, Keegan aside, was Sir John Hall. David, a local councillor and non-footy fan, simply could not understand why Brian and his socialist mates admired this man so associated with Thatcherism. David missed two points, namely, that this was football, not politics, and secondly, there was far more to Sir John than his previous admiration for some of Thatcher's work.

He believed in the region, and, in his own words, felt the Geordies were the Basques of England and that the club was fighting for the nation, the Geordie nation. He once dreamed of having a side with eleven Geordies in it, just like Bilbao, but that never came to pass. In the increasingly global age of football, an all-Geordie team was simply not possible.

Brian met John Hall at a Gateshead–Runcorn FA Cup tie. Brian managed to make a total misjudgement about the nonchalant claim of a young lad, who said he attended every match but did not have a season ticket. Brian naturally felt that the youngster was trying to talk up his Mag credentials, only for Grandad to come over and ask him if he wanted another coke. It was Sir John. A red-faced Brian exchanged some banter, and felt considerable guilt that he had ever doubted this lad's claims about his access to games without tickets. The region and Newcastle United were part of the same ticket for that visionary and passionate Grandad. He would later draw up plans for a major new stadium up from Leazes Park, encountering small but vociferous opposition from some groups including the Greens. This tested Brian's own green credentials, but Andy was fully behind the idea if a bigger stadium was needed.

At one point, the Gateshead councillors became extremely excited, when there was a possibility of the club moving to their Athletics Stadium, but this was never realistic. Newcastle United play in Newcastle - full stop.

Chapter Twenty-one

At the end of the Rainbow

During these years, United took the Premiership by storm, and quickly became a major force on the national stage. In their first season they finished third, banging in 82 goals. The following years saw them placed sixth, second and second. One of those runners-up places was to prove extremely painful. This was the era when the Mags could finally see that Rainbow and that elusive Pot of Gold at the end of it, and it only seemed a matter of time before the ultimate prize was seized.

When Keegan's side launched itself into the Premiership in 1993, after an initial stuttering start, a draw at Old Trafford at the end of August was the first sign that they would be far from out of their depth. The vast majority of Mags knew this, although there was some doubt at the national level. Brian heard of the draw in Edinburgh's Waverley Station, and received some rather strange looks from a set of Hearts fans as he waved his fist in the air. He rapidly assured them that his gesticulation was not directed towards them. The nation then saw the Toon Army, now the official title, in action on their SKY tv screens in September when Sheffield Wednesday were beaten 4-2 at St James, with Cole getting two, Mathie and Allen the others.

In November, Andy Cole did Brian a big

favour, when he destroyed the Red Scousers at Gallowgate in a 3-0 victory. Some kind of enquiry later occurred over the goalkeeping of Grobbelaar, but obviously nobody was aware of that at the time. Brian still does not care anyway, as beating Liverpool remains good enough for him, whatever the circumstances.

The return bout was even better. After years of humiliations and mocking from the locals, thousands of Geordies travelled to Anfield in April to see General Robert E Lee, and, yes, Andy Cole put two goals in, without reply from the home side. The lean and painful years down there were buried, or were for the time being, and brother Dave was uncontrollable. He had gone down with his fellow councillor Bryan, and they celebrated as if they had just won the Cup. Celebrations for the season's achievement were justified. The Mags had finished third, and were a force to be reckoned with. At the end of that month, Aston Villa went down 5-1 in face of the might of this side with flair and speed, and with Andy Cole completing a club record by reaching 40 goals in a season. Norman, brother Dave, Joe, and Brian, rocked inside St James, with every other Mag, as they sang *Andy Cole, Andy Cole, Gets the Ball, Scores a Goal.*

There was even icing on the cake. For the trip to Sheffield United, Brian, Jane, and Claire were visiting Barney and his family near York, and Brian had persuaded Barney to drive him down to Yorkshire's first [or is it second?] city. The stakes were high - qualification for Europe. The motorway near Sheffield was grid-locked, as half the Geordie nation was on it, in buses, cars, and dodgy-looking vans. Everybody had wanted a ticket for this, and brother Dave was with Mick and Paul, Fr Steve's brothers, in the United end, but Brian had to try other means to obtain access. He sat in that traffic jam, watching fellow Mags using the toilet facilities in the nearby fields and trees, much to the bemusement of traffic heading north, in growing anxiety. He could not afford to be late, as he had to collect two tickets – paid for, it should be stressed – from a Sheffield MP. Given the demand for entry, he had used alternative means to ensure that he saw the return to Europe.

He and Barney made it just in time, met the MP briefly outside the ground, and they were given a very strict warning not to show their colours and remain seated in the posh area right next to the Directors box. Very difficult conditions were attached to those tickets, but they adhered to them, well, until Newcastle got a corner in the third minute. As they rose up, so did half the posh section, thus confirming that the Geordie tribe will always use its many and varied contacts in order to get into a game. After some debate with the stewards, and possibly the Mayor, they were allowed to remain, as long as they created no trouble. They agreed, and watched their side qualify for Europe – or rather get beat, and still qualify for Europe. Arsenal did United a favour by winning a European trophy, creating room for entry into the UEFA Cup. Back in Europe, and back in the big time.

Sadly, by this stage in his life, Brian was beginning to develop a panic disorder which increasingly affected his travelling, and was to lead to a very debilitating condition in many situations. In the end, it brought with it a reliance on medication, and over-use of alcohol in a bid to deal with its effects. It was finally diagnosed as a form of PSTD - post traumatic stress disorder - related to Brian's domestic life in his childhood and early teens, and eventually led to periods off work and ultimately, full-scale incapacity.

Nevertheless, while he missed out on this venture onto the continent, and indeed others to come, he enjoyed it just the same. Plenty of his various mates became hardened European travellers, including Ian, Big Dave, the future Marion, whom he would meet in later years, and Bryan from Washington. Those early European games added extra buzz to the aura surrounding St James. The initial entry saw an incredible result away in Belgium, when Antwerp were destroyed. Five away goals were scored that night, further alerting the nation to the fact that Keegan was building something very special. Brother Dave came out with one of his familiar phrases: "Freddy is coming to get you." Not Shepherd of course, but Freddy Fletcher, the man who was working alongside Sir John Hall, and who shared a similar vision on the future of Newcastle United.

The pre-season tournament in Glasgow in the summer of 1994 reminded the side and the fans that they were not quite up to the standards of the world stage just yet. They beat the Mancs in the semi-final section in a penalty shoot-out - a very rare event indeed in modern NUFC history. It was particularly pleasurable for the Geordie following, which naturally outnumbered the opposition support. It would have been quite a journey from London, Cornwall, and Timbuktoo.

In the final, Sampdoria taught Newcastle a lesson in football. Brian saw the game in the Highlands town of Forres, where he was on holiday with his wife Jane and Claire. Coincidentally, he would watch United on tv in that town years later, when he was up there with his second wife Wendy. Brian met Wendy in Newcastle and discovered that Forres was her home town.

Brian took in the game at a pub near the RAF base at Kinloss. The place was full of NUFC, plus a drunken Rangers fan. At half time the landlady had a quiet word with him, as he was beginning to irritate the Geordie pilots, engineers and mechanics. At full time, Brian jumped in his taxi, arranged by the said landlady, to return to the holiday farmhouse up in the hills above Forres town. Unfortunately, the drunken Rangers fan staggered into the back – unfortunately for him, that is. The driver talked football, and ignored the rantings about Fenians and Glasgow Celtic.

Arriving at Brian's destination, the taxi driver winked as he dropped him off, asking for some paltry payment. The taximan added that he was a Celtic fan, and that the BlueNose, now asleep in the back, would pay the main fare when they arrived in the town centre - just next to the police station, in case his guest refused to pay the massive bill facing him.

On the European front, there was a meeting with the Basques when Atletico Bilbao came to town in October and were defeated 3-2. This was not quite enough to get United through as they went down in the return leg. It was enough though for free beer and food for Geordies when they landed in Bilbao. The

Basques had a fantastic time in the Bigg Market and elsewhere, and hit it off with their Geordie counterparts. Their reception was covered in their regional - or rather national - press, and the result was thousands of Geordies being treated like Kings and Queens by their hosts in the Basque country. This all had some small impact on Brian.

On a rare visit abroad some years later, he jumped in a taxi in that city, desperate to catch a train. The driver looked at his top, said NUFC, smiled, and belted through every back alley he knew in order to ensure that train was caught. Brian thanked him, and as he prepared to pay, the Basque stated, in broken English, that he was NUFC, and NUFC only had to pay a very small fare.

The League position in 1994-95 was a so-called disappointing sixth, but many a battle-weary Mag would have settled for that after years of failure under McGarry, McFaul, Gordon Lee, and even Joe Harvey. In October, Fat Baz from university days came up for one of his visits, following his beloved Blackburn. Strange events always seemed to take place whenever he landed for such matches. He spent one Saturday night in the Queen Elizabeth hospital, as Brian's poisoned finger was being lanced. Brian should have gone for attention earlier, but was at the match instead. Fat Baz naturally had no intention of holding his mate's hand for hours, and left the hospital for a drink in Deckham. He returned within the hour, opting for a seat in the hospital waiting room, rather than for a night out in Deckham.

On another occasion, a very strange event occurred, and has been erased from all

United history books, as if it never happened. Alan Shearer was booed at St James. He was wearing a Blackburn strip and he was a Geordie. Nobody admits to having committed this crime.

In early 1995 few realised that Keegan had plans for the final assault on the title. One incident in early January gave little indication of his thinking. Keegan shook Tyneside to the core by selling Andy Cole - to rivals, Manchester United. A group of Mags gathered outside the ground, and it seemed some kind of Romanian-style demonstration was under way. Keegan came out, and told them to keep faith. Most did, including Brian, Joe, and the rest, as they simply did not believe that their manager, or Sir John, were about to turn the clock back to the days of the Selling Club.

The fixture list brought Manchester United to St James just after the sale of Cole, but, on police orders, both he, and Gillespie, the winger coming in the opposite direction, were not allowed to play. Keegan got a fantastic reception and he deserved it. By the summer, Les Ferdinand was part of the squad, and the push for the Premiership crown was ready.

Chapter Twenty-two

Death of Two Dreams

The charge to the top took off at lightening pace. This side seemed unstoppable. Sir Lesley Ferdinand led the line, banging in goals which saw Joe flatten Brian on more than one occasion. Les's pair against Chelsea certainly resulted in some bruises. Beardsley, General Robert E Lee, Ginola, and the rest blasted other Premiership sides aside. Amidst this furious launch to the top of the table, a strange visitor arrived at Gallowgate, in the form of the Tory Prime Minister, John Major. Joe cannot recall any announcement that he was actually at the game, and given his grey personality, was probably unnoticed. Joe and Brian were annoyed that he had been given a No 10 Black & White shirt. Although Major was a Chelsea fan, his sport was cricket, a diversion which simply passes away the summer before football takes over again.

Brian's only interest in that sport had seen him arrive at Headingley on a Durham cricket club bus trip, and witness a fight between some of the bus trip and some Leeds United Nazis. One of the club's players was a black West Indian lad and the bus had taken offence. The racists were also Leeds anyway, so the offence was doubled. That bus trip ended in more problems, when a dispute between the NUFC and SAFC forced the driver to pull into the hard shoulder to get things

sorted. Cricket lover aside, of course, Major was
something far worse for many Mags - a Tory
Prime Minister.

Joe, Ian, and Brian later speculated upon
what would have happened at St James if Maggie
Thatcher had ever dared show her face. Given her
dislike for the region, it would have been
extremely unlikely that she would have done so,
but if she had, they agreed that Northumbria's
finest may well have had a very busy day. Visiting
Prime Ministers aside, the Black & White
juggernaut rolled on, and by Christmas glory was
on the horizon.

At this point, Brian's own horizon was
changing. Jane wanted Claire to have a garden,
and live in a nicer house. By late autumn,
prospective buyers of the Avenues property in
Bensham were coming and going. One left in a
very grumpy mood, mainly because Brian took
him up to the attic room to show him the view.
The wife seemed keen on the place, and the
husband was going along with it, until the would-
be seller opened the attic window to show him
the perfect view of St James across the river on
the hill. The bloke replied that he hated the Mags,
and the Red & White's interest in the house
collapsed. The place was sold though, and a
shambolic and disorganised shift, with the help of
Tarmac Nobby, one of those older Shiney Mags,
Mogga, Sam, and SAFC Nige, saw the family
ensconced in Oxclose, Washington, just before
Christmas.

By the spring of 1996, it was becoming
obvious that more change was on the way. There
had always been tensions between the couple.

One particular prophecy made by Jane a couple
of years earlier in a Low Fell pub was to come
true. A planned Easter holiday had to be delayed
for a day, as there was a match to take in, and
Brian felt it made little difference as they could
add an extra day on at the end of the break. Jane
tried to insist that he would have to miss the
game. He refused, and replied that NUFC were
part of his life long before he had ever met her.
She abruptly retorted that there was a good
chance they would be after she had gone. This is
not to blame the marriage difficulties on United –
that would be harsh on the club, and totally
inaccurate.

That spring in 1996 saw the marriage
collapsing, and by the late summer, Brian had
packed his bags and taken off for Low Fell. He
finally landed in Heaton, leaving behind his
lawnmower, which he had bought in an attempt
to save the marriage. She had wanted a garden.
Kev later suggested that whilst the lawnmower
was a noble attempt, it might have been a better
idea to have opted for diamonds and flowers.

Against this tumultuous and painful
background, life with NUFC continued, and many
will recognise that it could often help through
times of trouble. But life at Gallowgate was
becoming traumatic as well, brutally running
alongside the failing marriage. This was, after all,
the Year of the Missed Title. The twelve-point lead
crumbled, unravelled, and all watched on in
despair at its slow, and agonising erosion. That
gold pot at the end of the rainbow was stolen by
Manchester United, and Eric Cantona was one of
the main robbers, twisting a red knife into the

Black & White blood in early March at St James. The real United pounded the Manc goal in the first half, and Peter Schmeichel decided to give one of his best ever performances between those sticks, with the occasional help of the crossbar and goalposts.

It was 0-0 half time, and the mood in the East Stand toilets said it all. There was a kind of eerie silence, only broken by comments that this was not going to be the night for the Mags. Joe looked at Brian, just like Scotty looked at Brian before the Sunderland play-off six years earlier. It was as if they knew. Manchester had one attack in that second half. Cantona – 1-0.

There was still time to claw their way back up the side of the ship. Liverpool joined the party, and kicked the NUFC cat further down towards the sea, scoring a goal in the last minute at Anfield in their 4-3 victory. The game was labelled the best ever game of the Premiership, and the NUFC museum has some kind of plaque which states this to be the case. Bollocks! Best ever Premiership match for whom? Brother Dave, Ian, Father Steve, Kev, Gus, all of them, would have settled for the most boring 1-0 away win in history that night.

By April, Brian was leaving a pub car-park in Washington whilst Mags attacked Sunderland fans, and the sirens of the vans of Northumbria's finest echoed around the area. The SAFC had broken the unwritten law in divided lands, and had celebrated when Blackburn's Fenton put two killer goals in against United in the last few minutes of the match at Ewood Park, thus ensuring Batty's opener was meaningless. As

Brian walked one of the loneliest paths of his life, he thought about Fenton - a bloody Geordie. A bloody Geordie! Fenton's photo was immediately taken down from his home town Catholic Club in Whitley Bay, for very obvious reasons, and some still speculate to this day whether Fenton ever drinks in the Toon, and if so, what kind of sunglasses and false moustache he wears.

And so it all ended. Keegan made his defiant speech after Ferguson wound up him up for the Leeds game, and he was cheered to the rafters in yet another Washington pub, defiant to the end. "He Would Just Love It, Just Love It." So would have all the rest, but the Mancs took the title, and that pot of gold at the end of the rainbow.

Chapter Twenty-three

He's Coming Home!

The loss of the title was a massive blow. So near, so close. Summer was time to recover, and another interlude with England took up some of the time, on this occasion with the country acting as host to the European Nations Cup. As usual, Brian, Scotty, Ian, Mogga, brother Dave, and a lot of others were not particularly interested. Apart from watching some football, their thoughts were mainly on the season to come.

One England–Scotland match did cause a stir in the pub, when Peter, a Heaton Mag came over to Washington, and joined Brian and some of the others for the match. Peter was always a solid lad, fanatical NUFC, with a hatred of Arsenal, and a dislike of nationalist English over-hype. He never hid his strong opinions, and this led to Den and Lofty, the England pair, telling Brian that Peter would be going through the pub window at half-time unless he shut up. Brian used his diplomatic skills to calm the situation. He, Sam and Mogga were on Peter's side, but the other two understood that, accustomed to it over the years. Peter owes Brian for that intervention, only he probably does not know it.

The national radio was dominated by the song, *It's Coming Home, It's Coming Home, It's Coming, Football's Coming Home*. There was a far more important homecoming on the horizon, and this time it did not involve welcoming the team back after an FA Cup defeat. It involved the Lion of Gosforth, a certain Mr Alan Shearer. Much-needed sunshine came into Brian's life, extremely clouded by the imminent domestic split and the failed title campaign. Alan Shearer Was Coming Home. *He's Coming Home, He's Coming Home, Shearer's Coming Home.*

The Mag diaspora across the region, and the globe, went totally ballistic. Time again for jammed telephone lines, workplaces grinding to a halt, North East businesses losing profits, with the noteable exception of BT. Sir John and Keegan sat alongside the best centre forward in English, and possibly European football, and announced that he was coming home for a world record transfer fee. The icing on the cake, as if it was needed, was that Shearer had turned down the Mancs in the process.

This was a far bigger event than any England game in that European competition. Even Wendy, Brian's future partner, got entangled. She was a GP in Walker, had no interest in football, and one of her receptionists raced in and proclaimed: "Shearer's coming." Wendy thought he was a new patient. Meanwhile, Brian's new NUFC contacts in Felling allowed him access into the ground for the welcoming party, whilst 20,000 stood outside at the back of the new Leazes End. Dave, the owner of the Fox pub, took him, along with Kenny and Stewie to St James via a brewery pass. It would be ten years, with Jackie Milburn's goal record gone, before they all gathered in the ground to hear *Time To Say Goodbye,* and see sights of very big Geordie blokes with very big tattoos and very big necks crying like babies.

That was well into the future. For the present, it was yet another time when it just made it all worthwhile. The title would surely be on Tyneside, and revenge against the Mancs secured by the following summer. However, the quest for that revenge did not get off to a brilliant start. In August, the Geordie tribes gathered at Wembley for the Charity Shield fixture against their Red rivals. *He Turned You Down, He Turned You Down, Shearer Turned You Down*. Sir Alex Ferguson, who tended to like Newcastle fans, and once said that their fans deserved so much better, was in no mood for charity.

One of the tribe was on holiday with Jane and Claire in Ffestiniog village in North Wales, and sat with his six-year old daughter in an almost empty local pub to watch the match. Claire proudly sported her away purple hooped top, while Brian opted for straightforward Black & White. The only other people in the place were two blokes who said nothing, and a dozen or so Manc Gloryhunters from Cornwall, the West Midlands, and probably Timbuktoo. They shouted a lot, taking time out to mock and verbally abuse a seething father and daughter as the goals rained into the Newcastle net.

Brian made four misjudgements that day. The first was ignoring the fact that the game was at Bloody Wembley, the second was forgetting that NUFC had a history of not turning up when it mattered, and the third was that he did not know that the club had a history of Charity Shield disasters, having last won it against Northampton in 1909. To be fair, not a lot of people know that.

The fourth mistake could have been far more dangerous indeed. Young Claire was nearly in tears after their fourth goal and asked her Dad if she could go out and play on the swings, which were visible from the bar. As soon as she left, Dad let rip at the foul-mouthed Reds, and demanded if they normally shouted foul-mouthed abuse at bairns. They did not like his reaction, sang *Sad Geordie Bastard,* and a couple of them began look to look menacing. Brian felt anxious, not because of their threats, but because he had clearly abandoned his parental duty if he was about to be assaulted. Years later, Claire would probably have joined in, but she was bit young for that at the time.

And then, for perhaps the only moment in his life, he was relieved to hear Scouse accents. The two quiet blokes in the corner – they looked as if they were on the run from Walton Jail - said their first words of the day. They pointed out that they were Sad Scouse Bastards who agreed with the Geordie. The Plastic Mancs looked terrified, rightly so, and shut up. Not all Scousers were bad, thought Brian, and he returned home, not mentioning the incident to Jane.

Claire was a vital part of Brian's whole life now, and shortly after the North Wales holiday, her parents finally split. In the late autumn, after a stay in Low Fell, he moved in with a friend, Wendy, who was later to become his second wife. By early 1997 Claire was spending half of her time with her Dad in the Heaton flat. Two years later she was joined by another gorgeous, precious baby Mag, Kirsty. Special K, as she became known, made her appearance at the

RVI in town. As always, the latest addition to the United world knew little of her Black & White fate, even though it impacted upon her whilst she was still in the hospital itself. Newcastle were by then playing a European tie away to Sofia in Bulgaria. The maternity ward visitors and some of the staff took time off from smiling at the babies to nip along the corridor and catch up with events in Eastern Europe. Naturally, her doting Dad stayed at Kirsty's bedside – well, most of the time anyway.

Brian euphoric at birth of daughter
- another Mag

During this period, Brian's office had long since moved from the Gateshead end of the Tyne Bridge to Felling, or the Felling, as it is known. Through his own choice, he switched from researcher to caseworker, which brought him into daily contact with the local people and their wide-ranging problems. Work in Felling introduced a new set of Mags into his life. Kenny and Stewie had gone with him to the Shearer Homecoming. Kenny was a larger-than-life character with strong opinions and an endless desire to analyse, predict and dissect, the set-up at NUFC. His son was a Mag. No choice again, except his life was more difficult than most youngsters, as he lived with his Mam in Kildare in Ireland, and his school was dominated by Manchester United, Liverpool, and Celtic fans. He wore his top with pride, and once sat next to Brian at a match, only to embarrass the latter with his superior knowledge of the game and his insistence that Brian put his cigarette out. He was only nine at the time. Stewie was a more studious fan, with a dislike of Manchester United. Young Barry was a fanatic too. The venue was the Fox in Felling, and football was always high on the agenda.

The Black & White side of life had seemed fine though back in that summer of 1996. All soon recovered from that public mauling in the Charity Shield. With Shearer at the helm and Keegan in charge, the next title push was ready to begin. Very few realised that one man had not recovered - Keegan. It all set off as planned, and in the early stages there seemed little sign of trouble ahead. September saw a rather bizarre derby take place at Roker Park, as under police orders, no Mags were allowed in the ground. Joe, Ian and Brian took in the match inside the Arena in town, where the game was relayed onto a giant screen.

The victorious Newcastle goals were greeted in silence over in Sunderland and with euphoric scenes inside the Arena. The three friends enjoyed the strange occasion, which had been rendered even more strange by the sight of hundreds of NUFC singing at the screen. Every time the Mackems had sang a song, those Mags had responded vociferously. Joe pointed out that Roker Park might not just have been able to have heard any of these responses.

The same month saw Claire have her baptism at St James, officially becoming a member of the Church but not always able to attend the mass itself. Joe, who regarded her as a proxy niece, moved seats to Kev's vacant one – he was living abroad – to let her to sit next to her Dad. She saw a pulsating 4-3 victory against Aston Villa with Shearer and Sir Les amongst the scorers. Young Claire was held up in the air on four occasions, and patted by the couple from Chester-le-Street and the headmaster from Morpeth who later sadly died at a young age. He was a quiet, calm sort of bloke, assessing games with intelligence, until he lost his tranquility whenever a United goal hit the net.Claire was surrounded by a group who had all got to know each other by then. After this result, they demanded that she return to every game.

That group in the East Stand got to know each other over the years. Joe was there of course, occasionally replaced by Big Shaun, his son, or Bob, his brother-in-law. Over the years Joe would sometimes make the ultimate sacrifice for

Brian and shift from his treasured seat, moving
further along the stand in order that Claire could
sit next to her Dad. As she grew older, he would
abandon this policy, although it did not bother his
proxy niece as she was just happy to be in the
ground. Aside from the quiet Headmaster, the
seats nearby included his mate, who turned out to
hold down a big job in a bank in the town. He
was far less calm, and never needed a goal to set
him alight. Two ultra-loyal brothers sat in front.
They resented of some of the whinging which
occurred around them, and made their feelings
known. Ray and his wife from Chester-le-Street sat
behind Brian, and she was possibly one of the
most passionate of all the seat-dwellers.

Two Boldon lads were slightly
unpopular, not because of their characters, but
because of their annoying habit of arriving late -
every match. And finally there was the bloke from
Tow Law, who constantly accused the team of
going the wrong way, even though they were
normally going the right way. This caused Joe,
and more so Claire, much amusement.

After her home debut against Aston Villa
that September, Claire was naturally unable to get
into the ground regularly. A month later, and her
Dad could not get in either. He was sharing his
ticket that season with Ian, as a result of the
financial pressures of separation. At the beginning
of the season, as they sat at a table in Gateshead
Civic Centre, Ian had suggested that it was only
fair for Brian to choose first in game selections.
He promptly shouted Sunderland home, and Ian
promptly shouted Man U home. Actually, he
shouted Manure. Ian is many things, but as far as

anybody knows, he is not a qualified soothsayer, yet it was as if he could see into the future that day.

Two months later, Ian was in the ground, and Brian was in the Star on Westgate Road, watching the glorious, exhilarating 5-0 demolition of Manchester United, which led to the video which Kev and many others still watch to this day. This was the revenge for the title loss and the Charity Shield, as Ferguson's side were destroyed and humiliated. *Philippe, Philippe Albert, Everybody Knows His Name,* placed possibly the best chip over a keeper ever seen, certainly in the history of Newcastle anyway. The ground, and the Star, went berserk, and Brian felt little regret about his foolish choice. The euphoria and joy overcame any such negative feeling.

A few days later, after United had done their duty, Brian had his own duty to do, by saying a few words at the funeral of Auld Matty over in Saltwell crematorium. He first met the World War veteran in a Gateshead cafe opposite the Trafalgar pub years earlier on his way to work, and he learned much from him over morning cups of coffee. Matty had several claims to fame, not least one which had seen him as a referee between England and Scotland troops in a match just a few miles down road from the Japanese in Burma. He was chosen on the grounds that the Geordie would be neutral, and his fellow soldiers agreed, as they did not feel he was either English or Scottish.

Matty told Brian all about Hughie Gallacher and the Journal headline on his tragic death: "Hughie of the Magic Feet is Dead." Matty would also go into great detail about Jackie Milburn, Len White, and the three FA Cup final triumphs of the 1950s. He often made Brian late for work, but gloomily predicted that those days would never return. At his funeral, Brian pointed out that Matty had passed away a few days before the Philippe Albert chip, and that he would have regretted that. Matty was smiling from That Place Up Above – at least Brian hoped so.

After that Manc slaughter, Keegan's side began to hiccup and hit a relatively bad spell on the pitch. This was rectified just after Christmas, and brought with it another NUFC earthquake. It was a bombshell. Newcastle hammered Spurs 7-1, but this was not the bombshell. That came soon after when Keegan walked, and shocked the Geordie nation to its very core. He was grey and ashen-faced and he had given it his all, but The Lost Title had finished him off, along with perhaps some other factors. He gave the fans the dream, and he had lived it with them, and most will never forget that.

A new King was brought in as manager, this time Kenny Dalglish. There was a Cup disaster, when Brian took Claire into the lower paddock to see a home defeat to Nottingham Forest. Both were taken aback, partly due to the defeat, and partly due to the view from right next to the touchline which gave another perspective on the pace and strength required in the modern game. Forest just had more of those qualities that day, and it was to be the last FA Cup home defeat for a decade, when the Plastic Geordie Manc Steve Bruce brought Birmingham to St James in 2007 and humiliated the Toon in front of millions of BBC viewers.

In 1997, however, that Cup tie was seen as a blip, as Kenny steered Newcastle into second place in the Premiership. A thrilling game took place in February, when Shearer hauled United back from a 3-1 deficit at St James to a 4-3 victory. Brian saw the match in a tiny pub near Harbottle in deepest Northumberland. On a week's holiday with Wendy and Claire, he enquired at the local post office and the pub where the SKY game would be available, and was told that a small hamlet a couple of miles away usually put games on. He checked this out by visiting the place with Claire. Having ordered two orange juices and a packet of crisps at opening time, he asked the owner if the match was on in the evening. The latter reacted like an old Border Reiver being questioned about the whereabouts of some of his clan. What match? No match here, marra.

Fortunately, his wife emerged from the kitchen, having overheard the exchange, and asked Brian if he was a proper supporter. He confirmed that he was a season-ticket holder and was only in the area because of a cock-up over the fixture list. She turned on her husband, called him a daft bugger, and told Brian to come back on the night. It turned out that they piped SKY down into the bar illegally and the landlord suspected the visitor, wearing a Black & White top and jeans, was an undercover SKY agent. Rupert Murdoch's people were apparently cracking down on such showings across Northumberland, but Rupert must have been desperate if he was prepared to send out characters wearing strips accompanied by their bairn. It was worth it, just to see that tremendous recovery on the pitch. The landlady even arranged for a local farmer to drop the guest off back in Harbottle, which was kind of her, but proved hairy, as drink-driving laws did not seem to operate in that area.

March saw another 4-3 result, this time against the Scousers at Anfield – again, and a defeat – again. It could not compare with the 1996 version in hurt and pain, but was galling nevertheless. John, a Sunderland fan, sat quietly alongside Brian and others as they swore at the telly at the Hotspur in the Haymarket. It did not affect any push for the title, as second place was the target by now, and Kenny took United into it, and the qualification stages of the Champions League. There had been a sniff of glory in Europe, but sadly had been ended in mid-March in a UEFA Cup quarter-final against Monaco, lost 0-4 on aggregate. Another lonely and despondent night after the 3-0 defeat in France, but by the end of the season, there was always the Champions League to look forward to.

As the summer drifted on, there seemed little sign of trouble to come, yet it came with a bang, beginning with yet another eventful summer. Dalglish was sadly dismantling some of the Keegan side, and he managed to cause total consternation at a wedding celebration in the Yorkshire Dales. Brian, Wendy, and John and Gina, a fanatical Mag couple, were relaxing in the late afternoon. John was hugely devoted to NUFC, so much so that he left his own wedding to pop over to a home match and returned for the evening disco. This was with the blessing of Gina, who naturally understood and thought nothing of it.

At the Yorkshire wedding, however, relaxation was soon turned into panic, as John learnt that Shearer had gone down in total agony in a pre-season friendly. This later turned out to be caused by a broken leg and serious ankle ligament damage. That was bad enough, but the club had just sent Sir Les to Spurs, and were now begging him not to return. He refused, and the fans understood. No bad words about Les Ferdinand are permitted.

Chapter Twenty-four

Eva Peron was right

The new season did not start badly, despite this disastrous background. Brian's birthday times with NUFC were rarely dull. In August, two days before yet another birthday, the team were playing Croatia Zagreb in the vital away leg of the Champions League qualifier. He and Claire took in this match from possibly the best view ever of an away game – in a holiday cottage next to a loch near Oban. There was no bloody Channel 5 in the house, so they settled for listening to the game on a radio with extremely poor reception. Wendy wisely opted for a walk, as the pair paced, danced, and jumped around the room in full view of boat-owners looking on in total bemusement, probably assuming that some strange kind of local ritual was under way. Then came Temuri Ketsbaia's goal which earned the necessary 2-2 draw, sending the Oban cottage and Geordieland into ecstasy.

It was time to concentrate upon the League, and the holiday car raced back on the Saturday night to Heaton, in order to ensure that Dad and daughter could watch the SKY away match at Liverpool on the Sunday. They put their strips on the next morning, crossed over the road into the newsagents, and bought their Sunday Sun, only to be told that the game had been cancelled. Cancelled? The newsagent informed

Brian that Lady Diana had been killed in a car crash the previous evening. He thought it sad that two young sons had lost their mother, but like one half of the country, would not join the mass hysteria which swept Britain for the week. Returning home, he told Wendy the news – about the death, and the match being off – and she put the telly on.

The coverage spoke of the loss of a parent, and Brian noticed that Claire was retreating into the kitchen in tears. He followed her, as it was only a year after the marriage split, and tried to console her with advice about mothers and fathers. She interrupted him sharply, telling him that her tears had nothing to do with parents, and everything to do with the match being off. This sentiment was also held by many other Mags, including Joe who boomed in on the telephone, angry at news of the cancellation.

Attention soon returned to Europe. The Champions League was the big time for the big club. And it came no bigger in the form of Barcelona arriving at Gallowgate in mid-September, with Tino Asprilla destroying the Catalans with a hat-trick. Unfortunately, they pulled two back, but this did not dampen the wild scenes inside the ground and beyond. Brian, Joe, Scotty, Ian, and all the others had the time of their lives that night. Scotty had taken Tracey with him, as a wedding anniversary gift. Brian only just made it. It was bad enough missing the 5-0 against the Mancs in 1996, but absence from this one would have been too much to bear. His presence was a result of diplomatic negotiations with Wendy, as the game fell into the first week of a fortnight's holiday in Cornwall.

Naturally, Brian had no intention of missing this game, but confrontation was avoided, thanks to a wedding celebration being held two days after Barcelona. Bill, a solid local councillor and devoted Mag, was holding his do on the Friday night at the Irish Centre, and both he and Sally were very close friends of Wendy's. She agreed that a few days in the Lakes would be fine, with a return to Newcastle on the Wednesday, a visit to the wedding disco on the Friday, and a week in Cornwall just after.

Brian remains grateful to Bill and Sally to this day for getting married in that September. Familiar faces were present, including aforementioned John, the man who left his own wedding for a game, and NUFC talk was aplenty amongst them, most of it focusing upon a detailed analysis of the Barca triumph.

In November, the Champions League cancelled Bonfire Night, or at least it did in Newcastle. United were at home to Eindhoven, and it was live on tv. United lost, and so did the Guy Fawkes celebrations. A centuries-old tradition was moved to the following night, as it was rightly believed that most of the city would be in the house watching the football or at the match. Wendy was slightly shocked to learn the news, but only slightly, as she was becoming used to the Tyneside religion and its impact upon daily life and events. As her life with Brian developed, she would become more so. Children's birthday parties were arranged to fit around a match, and holiday plans generally made to avoid missing games.

Guy Fawkes has to wait

On the Premiership front, Kenny's side struggled, and eventually finished a disappointing thirteenth. It had been a few years since United were that far from the top zone, but there was another show in town in the form of the FA Cup. The nation wanted United out, after a row about playing at Stevenage for crowd safety reasons. The game duly took place there, and Ian told Brian that the Gateshead Corporation Club, or the Corpy as it affectionately known, was letting the kids in upstairs, so Claire squeezed into melee. They held the non-league side to a draw, and the returning Shearer finished them off in the replay.

The Cup run was up and running, all the way to Old Trafford and a semi against Sheffield United. The stands containing the NUFC shook to their foundations, which was a rare event at the ground of the 60,000 Muppets as Mags affectionately called the Red inhabitants of the Theatre of Dreams, or of GloryHunters that is. Scotty's house was now the traditional venue for matches, and Brian, forced to sell his ticket because of his panic disorder problem, joined him, Tracey, and Biffa the Dog. The boxer dog later appeared in Mad Mick's Toon Army fanzine, wearing a Black & White strip, with a note underneath stating "Biffa from Walkergate." His normal habit for a tv game was to fall asleep when it started, wake up at half time, and fall asleep again until full time. Other Mags have been known to have done the same thing on occasions, but even Biffa stayed awake for the semi. He sensed the anxiety, the tension, and joined in the wild celebrations when Shearer banged in that goal.

The climax to the show was, well, an anti-climax, with the predictable non-show, this time against Arsenal. A normal day at Wembley really, with the Geordies again out-singing the opposing fans. At one stage they resorted to shouting *Attack! Attack!* as their team seemed to have a fear of crossing the halfway line. Then came the predictable and traditional Homecoming – again. The team bus rolled into the town centre from Gosforth, with thousands of fans lining the route and packing out the area around the Civic. Even Wendy came down, and for the first, and last time, actually put on a discreet yellow NUFC top. Claire painted her face Black & White.

Once again, it was apology time from the club, and defiance time from the fans. *The Geordies, United, Will Never Be Defeated,* as the song goes. Some of the players looked gutted, but only some, unlike 1974, when they had all seemed ashamed and broken.

Still, a Champions League run, and an FA Cup final appearance, however disappointing, were hardly the stuff of total disaster, despite the increasingly dull team that Dalglish was building and the poor league finish. It was hardly Bedford, Hereford, or the Sunderland play-offs of the distant past. The summer saw the arrival of Stephane Guivarc'h, supposedly a fantastic French striker, and led to some NUFC support for France in the World Cup. There is some tradition in this tendency, as Brian and others have been known to follow Columbia (Tino Asprilla), Ireland (Shay Given), and Peru (Nobby Solano) for brief periods. The new French signing managed to score against the Red Scousers on August 30th, but the only problem was that it was in a 4-1 defeat at home.

Another character is worthy of mention. Sometime in 1988 a Brian was signed. His surname was Pinas, this caused some stick, so to speak, for Brian from some of his United mates. A new character, Graham, had emerged. He longed for the day when Pinas might lob Seamen, the Arsenal goalkeeper, especially in a live TV commentary. It never happened, as Pinas did not live up to expectations.

August 98 had already brought chaos with it. King Kenny was dethroned, sacked after a poor game against Charlton Athletic. Yet again, lack of forward planning from the club was in evidence. The sacking itself provoked intense dissatisfaction for Graham, the new United fanatic in the life of Brian. He was employed as a volunteer in the office, as he sought out his career as a researcher in politics. He immediately impressed Brian with his dedication, when he spent a whole afternoon devoting himself to the construction of a letter - about the treatment of Kenny Dalglish. Graham would clearly go far, and often did, to various away games with a shifty bunch from Rowlands Gill and Winlaton. He was a very useful addition to the office, as he was always willing to participate in debates – about Newcastle United of course. He was also keen to talk about his own time in care work when he had met an old man who had seen the great Hughie Gallacher play.

Graham was always ready to respond when provoked about the fact that his very early childhood was spent in Mansfield, and therefore he should have supported his home club. His family, shades of the Keegans, had left the region looking for work in the East Midlands pits. Economic refugees, Graham proclaimed, and he had only lived there for two years before they returned to North West Durham, but he always rose to the bait. His other claims to fame included predictions that the right-back Andy Griffin would become a superstar – which he did not – and that he was one of the hardcore who had been at Bournemouth in some league disaster. Graham failed to add that he was only living 30 miles away at the time.

Graham's disappointment with the sacking of Kenny Dalglish aside, hopes soared when his replacement arrived in the form of the legendary Ruud Gullit, a former fabulous Dutch international. He promised supporters sexy football. Scotty, brother Dave, Gus, and most of the rest, took the Black & White optimistic drug again. One of the biggest names in world football would surely take the club to that elusive trophy. After all, Gullit's whole career was littered with trophies. Gullit did not produce any league success, and even he began to question whether the club was cursed. Allegedly, the Dutchman visiting the local priest to see if some kind of exorcism could take place near the old hanging site. Tensions began to emerge with the disgraceful treatment of General Robert E Lee, who was not even given a shirt number, much to the disgust of supporters and not least Alan Shearer.

Once again the FA Cup show was back in town and once again, it was time to visit Biffa the Dog in Scotty's sitting room. Again, Biffa stayed awake to watch Big Al sweep Spurs aside at a bouncing, euphoric Old Trafford. Away from Biffa's sitting room, Scotty and Brian were unaware that Gus was stuck in Disneyland, Florida, trying to keep check on the score. When he heard the news, he visited a local liquor store but was refused alcohol as he had no ID. He was 42. They did add that he could buy a gun if he wanted, and failed to see the funny side when he said he would only have bought that if Newcastle had lost. A month later, he wished he had bought the bloody thing.

Still, after that semi-final, glory was on the agenda again and only Manchester United stood in the way. The Wembley script went to plan, Alex Ferguson's plan that is, and a re-run of the previous year took place. Some of those players

In Florida, Gus is refused booze but is offered a gun

representing United seemed to care even less than the ones the year before. Shearer did, and later expressed his view that he was pleased to see the back of that old stadium, a sentiment shared by thousands of his Geordie compatriots. It was deja vue time again, as the song goes, *Don't Expect This Love Affair to Last,* referring to the life of Eva Peron. For modern-day Geordie fans, that sentiment applies to BLOODY FA CUP AFFAIRS.

Claire painted her face Black & White for the traditional Homecoming. This time, Brian trooped into town, still defiant but beginning to get tired of this tradition of fanatical supporters welcoming home a team that had not turned up when it mattered. He was sitting on an invitation from some of his Newcastle political contacts which gave access to the private reception for the players, and he had no intention of using it. Looking at his daughter and observing her enthusiasm, he changed his mind, and overcame his inner depression. She would love to meet her heroes, even though most of them were not heroes at all. She still has the photographs, one sitting next to Temuri Ketsbaia. He was famed for his self-propelled launch into the Gallowgate advertising boards after one of his goals. Ketsbaia did seem to care, and he was brilliant with the kids.

Claire also got the autograph of another player, who did not care at all: Hamann, who later left for the Scousers. Dad and daughter had several discussions as to whether that autograph, and the photo with him, should be binned. Dad pointed out, against his real instincts, that the German did play in the World Cup. It is still with Claire somewhere, but obviously just buried deep in her bedroom and not on display. The Temuri photo is far more visible, but naturally not on the scale of the Shearer autograph obtained by brother Dave.

Away from St James, Brian's life was changing too. After Kirsty's arrival on the scene in September 1999, he changed his working hours for a spell, and ended up going to toddlers' groups in Jesmond and Byker. The mothers in the latter area were far more welcoming than the former, who despite their would-be lower middle class liberal views, seemed to find it hard to accept a man in the room. The Byker women never blinked. Brian spent some of his time watching Kirsty, and some of his time reading the back page of the Journal.

He was joined two years later by yet another wonderful baby Mag, this time, Becky. Officially her name was Rebecca, and both Brian and Wendy agreed, for different reason, that her name would never be shortened to Becks, as in Beckham. It never has been, and never will be. The two younger sisters later received knitted dolls from an Aunt in Scotland, with Black & White strips and hats. The dolls are both called Maggie.

The family had long since moved to a different part of Heaton, next to the park. Yet more United fans emerged, none more so than Ray the Barber. Brian had always thought Phil the Barber, back in Shiney, was the best at his trade. After the obligatory query into his courting and holiday plans, he would discuss United for the rest of the haircut, much to the annoyance of any listening local SAFC. Ray in Heaton simply cut out the questions on courting or holidays, and got straight to the main subject. Any glance into his shop confirms that this was inevitable. It was, and still is, decorated in black and white – signed photos, images of players in mirrors, you name it. Brian always enjoyed a visit to that barber's.

Claire however did not enjoy the company of Gordon, a lad from Dundee who now followed NUFC avidly, and would stop for some crack. This was fine for Dad, but it always interrupted the football game on the green and thus irritated daughter immensely. The milkman from Washington was a character too, as he lost considerable money collection time when he called at the house. He used to stand on the step for about 15 minutes contemplating any imminent fixture, or any recent defeat.

Job-wise, life as a caseworker continued, and Brian used to like to get into the office early via Byker or Dean taxis. You can guess the main topic of conversation. Brian's political connections did at least bring one major success for him. It took place at Gallowgate itself, when a match was organised involving a North East Eleven against a group of Westminster MPs. Kirsty and Claire got on the pitch with their strips on, and their Dad took the chance to score into an empty net at the Leazes End. MP Joyce held the baby Becky in her arms, whilst Brian belted that glorious goal into the net after a brilliant pass from Claire. The match had long since finished, there was no other player in sight, but that was not the point.

Chapter Twenty-five

Gods of Thunder

Back in 1999, the month of August had produced more upheaval. Gullit left, and to his credit, did not take with him a few million quid, unlike a certain other character in the future. It all exploded on a night of high drama and of even higher Geordie gloom. The Dutchman took on Shearer, and Big Duncan Ferguson as well, and dropped them both for a home game - against Sunderland. Leaving Big Dunc out was one thing, given that his only real affinity with the region was his pigeon-racing hobby, and for some, his time spent in a jail. Leaving out Big Al was quite another thing for a derby match and the SAFC following danced with joy at the news. The night sky was dominated by thunder, lightning and torrential rain, and all looked on as the Mackems won 2-1.

Their fans gleefully mocked the Mag hordes as the latter dejectedly wandered off to the pubs and clubs to drown their sorrows. Ian, Brian, and some of the others gathered in the Irish Centre, drenched to the skin, angry and distraught. Little did they, or the SAFC, know that the result had just done United one very big favour. In that penalty shoot out at the OK Corral between Big Al and Gullit, there was now only one winner, and the rest is history. A wonderful new dawn was on the horizon.

Managerial speculation took off amongst the group, and birthday time, or the day after that it, saw the Mags hammered at Old Trafford 5-1 on August 30th. Shortly afterwards, the town went crazy. Another Geordie was coming home, a County Durham Mag to his core, although some NUFC actually do not accept such backgrounds as qualification for Geordie Mag status. It was of course Bobby Robson. He used to journey up to Gallowgate from Langley Park, an old pit village and no doubt a divided one in terms of North East football. He had moved on to less glamorous places like Porto, and Barcelona, and of course had managed England, suffering the venom of some Mags who resented him dropping Keegan in 1982 and not picking Peter Beardsley automatically in 1986.

As ever, all that was forgotten. A Mag was back in town. By mid-September, Robson's first home game saw Claire hurled eight times towards the Newcastle sky, as Shearer hammered in five, and they won 8-0 against Sheffield Wednesday. The group were in cloud nine, taken up there by Bobby, and would stay there for some considerable time. By January, talk of relegation was finally buried as the Mags slaughtered Southampton 5-0 at the Cathedral, and the new saviour Bobby took United to a mid-table position by the end of the season.

Thus began the Robson era. His after-match talks, live on television in the Irish Centre and everywhere across Tyneside, were always met with silence, like some kind of major government announcement, almost in an atmosphere as if the nation was about to go to war. The Geordie nation was, and Bobby took the Mags back to the days of Keegan and major contender status. As Bobby prepared for another assault on the Premiership, the season opened with the biggest crowd seen at Gallowgate for many, many years. At last, there was room, or nearly anyway, for the fans, as 51,000 piled into the ground for the Derby County game.

This may have been the match where there was one empty seat, which apparently remained so until Christmas. One caring wife had bought her husband a season ticket, and presented it to him on December 25th. The said husband was not amused. However, Sir John's dream, although derailed in Leazes Park, was complete. There was now a true Cathedral on the Hill, seen for miles around, dominating the city skyline. The whole rebuilding process had seen scenes over summers with people taking photos or simply milling around, watching the building work in progress. It was certainly a different kind of way of spending a summer holiday.

In his first season, Bobby proudly led United to Wembley again. It was a semi-final against Chelsea, as the FA by now were staging such games at that dreadful place. A unique event had occurred during this Cup run, back in December. A replay brought Spurs back to Gallowgate, only for Brian to miss the game due to a baby-sitting commitment. Wendy's annual Christmas outing coincided with the match, and there was no way out. Brian loved his little baby Kirsty, but this was an extreme sacrifice in terms of marriage harmony, compounded by the fact that United won 6-1. Brian admits that the noise of his radio may well have distracted him from the monitor designed to check the offspring's breathing.

At that later visit to Wembley, for a change they were not humiliated, and actually scored a goal in the 2-1 defeat, with Robert Lee, restored into the camp, achieving it. No shame this time as they battled with dignity and courage, in true Bobby style. Brian, still disabled by his panic disorder and travel phobia, did brother Dave a favour and gave him his ticket. Dave was now living in Eastbourne and was driving the disabled Sunderland fan to their away games. Well, it was a favour, until some character spiked Dave's drink. After three pints he was taken into the police/medical centre at the stadium, suspected of being drunk and disorderly. They had all been so over various years, but brother Dave was innocent this time, and a medical examination proved it.

The group's venue in the Robson era was now firmly established at the Tyneside Irish Centre just down from the ground. Long gone were the days in the Printers Pie, the Trent House, the Star, and the Strawberry. In the Irish Club, Ian was by now very much a major player for the fans. He was in charge of the season ticket books, and established a solid reputation of being able to deliver for away fixtures. Kev re-emerged after his period of exile in Italy and the USA, although he was still in a kind of exile, living in London. Fr Steve was able to fly in from his Dublin base. Gus, Scotty, Brian, and all the others, sat there, usually in a spirit of hope and contentment as Bobby's side impacted upon the higher end of the

Premiership.

Other characters chipped in too. Piper was still around, as was Claire, but new faces appeared, including Mick the Sailor and his wife Lesley. Mick was often replaced by his son or daughter as he sometimes found himself in the middle of the China Sea or off the Norwegian coast. This annoyed him considerably if there was a big game in town. There was Carla, Ian's daughter, and the large family of Patricia from Gateshead days; John the Felling councillor and Big Dave, Nick and all the rest, including his brother-in-law, Stevie, who was a serious and accurate analyst, and SAFC hater. Brian worked with some of them. There was also Terry, that man with the most Black & White house in town, with his repertoire of songs from Leazes End days. Only Graham was missing. He was a Star man on Westgate Road, which was unfortunate for him. During one spell when his girlfriend was living opposite the pub, she could see him standing outside waiting for opening time.

The seasons rolled by with Bobby, as he re-established United as a major force near the top of the Premiership, although never came quite as close as King Kev had. Some of his signings were poor ones, but the presence of Bellamy, Robert, and others, brought flair and pace back to the Mags. One New Year, in 2001, saw Brian up in Forres in North East Scotland, in the house of Kenneth and Mary, Wendy's parents. Kenneth simply could not understand why people were interested in 22 men chasing a round ball around for 90 minutes. He was astonished when Brian retired to the kitchen, and Wendy suggested that

it was best not to disturb him. United were at
Spurs, they had Solano sent off, and lost 4-2.
Kenneth made one appearance to put the kettle
on, and seemed totally baffled that the normally
polite son-in-law was pacing around his kitchen,
with a radio on at full blast, talking to himself and
swearing. He quickly made his cup of tea, and
retreated to the sitting room. They normally talked
politics, but there was no conversation after the
game. Mary at least understood the importance of
Newcastle United in his life, and Wendy noted
that this was normal behaviour. Not a moment for
political chat, or any chat really, and the son-in-
law soon took off for his bed.

At one stage in this era, at the opposite
end of the country, Brian found himself accused
of lack of patriotism by a big Chelsea fan at Kings
Cross, on the basis that Alan Shearer had
announced his retirement from the English
national team in order to concentrate upon his
Newcastle career. In 2001, he had suffered yet
another major injury, and he felt that, after
recovery, there was only one nation he wanted to
represent, and it was not the English one. Brian
had missed the train, went into the station bar for
a pint, and came across the big Cockney who
launched a blistering assault on the famous
Number 9. Brian could accept accusations about
his own lack of patriotism – he could not care less
about England results – but defended the Lion of
Gosforth, pointing out that he had given his all for
Ingerland, and was often blamed for their defeats
anyway. He added that every Geordie he knew
preferred a fit Shearer playing for the Toon, and
felt that playing for NUFC was so more important

than playing for the Cockney's country. The Chelsea fan moved away, muttering some comment that Geordies were not English anyway. Precisely, thought Brian.

In August 2001, Brian's long-planned holiday arrangements led to a major cock-up. He and Claire found themselves in Oban, and not at St James, for the derby against Sunderland. They trawled the local pubs, and were finally directed to one which would definitely have the match on screen. It ended in a 1-1 draw, with Bellamy and Philips scoring the goals, but the real significance was that this was the most peaceful derby ever witnessed by Brian. The place was full of North East holidaymakers, with children, and a truce was in operation – proof that the two sets of fans can sit together, although the draw probably helped. One SAFC looked agitated at the lack of violence, but his bad attitude was soon spotted, and dampened down, by one of his uncles. It was actually good to see this occasion, when, for once, the rivalry was not accompanied by violence.

It reminded Brian of another occasion outside the Strawberry, when a group of Mags attacked another group of Mags. They had witnessed an attempted assault on a Sunderland fan who was walking towards the ground with his very young son, and intervened to prevent the attack. They rightly felt that the attackers were crossing a line, and told them in no uncertain terms that they could either continue the fight with the Strawberry drinkers or go off and look for Sunderland fans without children. Wisely, they opted for the latter option.

A line of a different sort was crossed only a month after that August derby on the Oban pub screens. It was crossed by Mr Roy Keane, ably encouraged by Shearer. A thrilling match took place at St James, when Robert, Lee, Dabizas, and then, blissfully a winner from Big Al himself via a Manc defender's body, saw Newcastle defeat Keane and his mates 4-3. Claire was in Brian's seat, and he was further along in the East Stand. Kev was watching the game in a Helsinki bar full of Finnish Reds and his American mate marvelled at the atmosphere booming out from that SKY screen. It was intense, and became more so when Mr Keane, a very bad loser, tried to have a go at Big Al. The latter seemed unperturbed, seemed quite pleased actually, and said something to him. Off went Keane as the referee brought out his red card, and up went St James. Only Barney was disappointed that day, as he had arrived at Kev's house, only for his Dad to give him the wrong ticket number, thus ensuring that he was unable to get in.

At least Barney could see the photo which later appeared, and was placed in Brian's toilet, showing the two squaring up, and with the headline: "What Al Really Said to Keane." It suggested that he told the raging Cork man that one day he would manage Sunderland(!).

Chapter Twenty-six

Back to the Continent in Style

December 2001 was a very interesting month for two reasons. The first involved the debt that Brian owes Joe, who refused to give up his seat for Claire's Dad, thus allowing her to sit next to him but not her Dad. This meant that Brian had to move nearer to the Gallowgate in the East Stand. He had a perfect view of one of Alan Shearer's best ever goals against Everton, when he sent the stadium into ecstasy. This was good enough, but things got better when the infamous London Hoodoo was finally ended at Highbury. Newcastle had not won in the capital for years, yet took on Arsenal and defeated them. Joyce, Brian's boss, had a chance to go with Bryan, but foolishly declined. Marion and her son David were there, and the Toon Army went berserk, again to the bemusement of the locals. Uri Geller later claimed the credit for the victory, but it was down to Bobby's stars, and had nothing to do with the spoon bender.

2001-2 saw Champions League qualification. Robson took United onto the continent in style, and the club's name ranked high in European football talk. There had been one early stumble in this crusade, in the summer of 2001. A record crowd for the Inter-Toto Cup saw 1860 Munich pushed aside, and the final, guaranteeing entry into the UEFA Cup, did not appear to be a difficult game. The French side, Troyes, landed at Gallowgate, and proved to be a real Trojan horse, gaining an unexpected 4-4 draw and knocking Newcastle out on that bloody away goals rule. Generally though, this was an era of tremendous excitement, with Bobby taking his side across Europe, very much major players on the stage. Brian's increasing panic disorder meant that he could not get to any of those games away, but it did not stop him watching them on TV, or getting to St James.

In the first game of the Champions League in 2002, United lost away to Kiev 2-1 and a month later, lost at home to Feyenoord. This was a blow, but most of that match seemed to pass unnoticed by one of the Shiney NUFC, who found himself sitting next to a guest visitor, Pilar from Spain. A niece of Brian's old mate, Carlos, she had been desperate to see United live in the stadium. Her temporary stay on Tyneside was due to her desire to improve her English and she did depart with a very improved use of language, Geordie of course. She worked as a waitress and then in a law firm ran by a couple of fanatical Mags. Life on Tyneside taught her that, before she left for home, she had to get inside Gallowgate. She had seen the Quayside, the beaches, the Cheviots, Hadrian's Wall, but had not been to the most important place in the region.

Pilar's impact in the Irish Centre was, as usual, a powerful one, as she was a rather attractive and bubbly young woman. A sudden interest in all things Spanish broke out, and the Shiney lad was particularly pleased to learn that he was sitting next to her. She later admitted that she was not amused, as he never stopped talking to her, whilst she tried to concentrate upon the game. She left town a few months later, as a Mag, and her father, Manolo is the proud owner of a Black & White top, which he wears in Granada, and of the DVD showing Shearer's goals, which he watches regularly. Thus, more conversions to the Faith.

Many matches stand out from those Champions League days. Despite consecutive losses to Kiev, Feyenoord, and indeed Juventus, Newcastle, in typical style, stubbornly reversed the seemingly irreversible and won the rest. The scenes in Holland against Feyenoord were incredible, and they were equally incredible in one Quayside pub when Bellamy got the winner. Juventus triumphed in Kiev, with the help of a certain young man, Obafemi Martens, and qualification for the next stage was achieved. One bloke was sent flying under a table in that Quayside pub, and did not re-emerge for a considerable period. He eventually hauled himself up, carried out some kind of Indian ritual dance, and ran out into the street, hopefully not directly into the Tyne itself. The team were in the next round, but found the going just a bit too tough. In their last game in that group they earned a creditable 2-2 draw in Milan: no shame in that.

One match stands out even more so for Brian, and it was not only because the side were in that next round: 26th February 2003, a date etched on his mind. Bayer Leverkusen at home. Obviously he had to attend the match. Unfortunately, bad timing ensured that he also had to attend a medical clinic earlier in the day, as a nasty twist of fate saw him having the operation which halts the ability to produce further offspring. It was particularly complicated, with the tie due only a few hours afterwards. Naturally, he was anxious to get to it, the match that is, not the vasectomy. Just before going into the Shieldfield health centre, Brian made a fatal mistake by visiting his former workplace at the residential care for a footy chat with Scotty. Fatal, because he mentioned the reason for his visit, only for one of his best mates to tell the rest of the staff, who proceeded to tell him about the brutal reputation of the Doctor over the road. The allegations were totally unfounded of course, but did not help matters.

There was no NUFC talk at the care home, but during the operation there was a lot of NUFC talk, initiated by the nurse and the Doctor as a distraction technique. Only on this occasion, United were not at the top of his conversation agenda, as his attention was focused upon balls off a different kind. The nurse mentioned Nobby, which seemed particularly inappropriate. The Doctor asked him what he thought the score would be, and a silent Brian just kept his eye on the medical activity. Job done, football was back on his mind, and he asked them if he would be able to attend the match that night. The medical advice was that although he would have some discomfort, as long as he sat still and remained careful, it should not be too much of a problem.

Sensible words, but they missed two important points. Brian was not renowned for sitting still in a seat for 90 minutes, and his seat companion was Joe, shaped like a bear with a grip to match if any excitement broke out. It did, and victory was achieved. A happy night, but Joe inflicted, aided by others nearby, some pain on his mate, and Brian walked back, very, very slowly, to catch the others in the club. Worth it, he thought.

Around that time, there had been hope of an FA Cup run, but Lady Luck drew out Arsenal away in March. The Globe pub in Shieldfield was packed out with anticipation and anxiety in the air. The former emotion lasted nine minutes, after Pires scored in the second minute, and Bergkamp added the second in the ninth. After ten minutes or so, a crowd of late arrivals squeezed their way into the bar, singing of Cup glory, only to glance at the faces and at the TV screen. The singing stopped, and so did the Cup run.

By this time domestic life in Heaton was also in trouble. Painfully, the marriage with Wendy was in difficulty. As things worsened, Brian took a break from it all, and crossed the Irish Sea to see Fr Steve in Dublin. Breaks from most situations are possible, but somehow NUFC always manages to get in the way of things, even when they are not playing. Half the week saw Fr Steve and his guest checking Biffa's NUFC.com website, buying the tabloids, and telephoning some of their Black & White contacts. The club was once again on the front page, and not the back, of every British newspaper. There were serious allegations, which later proved to be unfounded, that some members of the brat-and-bling pack had been involved in some sordid party in a West End hotel – the London West End, that is – and there were accusations of rape.

Speculation dominated the air, Dyer was mentioned, Bramble was emerging as a suspect, and although nothing came of it, this caused distress for all Mags, including the pair supposedly relaxing in Dublin.

Brian saw one match during his Dublin visit, on TV, in a pub packed with Armagh and Tyrone fans, as the Northerners descended into the capital in their thousands to see the Irish Gaelic version of football and its Cup Final. The Tyrone captain was a superstar, their Local Hero, representing his home County. They had won nothing for years, so Brian was able to identify with them, and told the mixed and friendly gathering of his choice.

A Tyrone supporter groaned in anguish, pointing out that the last thing they needed was the support of a Newcastle United fan, given their track record. It seemed that the NUFC reputation travelled far and wide, but on this occasion, the right horse was backed. The Tyrone skipper made a powerful, emotional speech afterwards as he dedicated the triumph to all those fans who had waited so many years for that success. Brian wiped a tear from his eye, along with all the rest from County Tyrone, partly because it was a very touching moment, and mainly because he was thinking if only it had been Big Al and Wembley.

Chapter Twenty-seven

Jambos, Casuals & Gremlins

For a change, a Mag had backed the right horse, but there were several occasions when the wrong horse was picked, and the Gallowgate curse was inflicted upon third parties. One particularly stands out in a pre-match discussion in the Irish Centre. Some of the group, including Scotty and Gus, owe Hearts an apology. Discussing the Scottish Premier League, they decided that they would like Hearts to break the Glasgow monopoly, as they were sitting high in the table and it looked possible. Within a week, that club descended into chaos, with resignations everywhere, and the Jambos, as they are known, plunged towards disaster.

Back to the Easter of 2003, Brian stayed with Kev in London. The two old mates went their separate ways, Kev down the Thames, and Brian to Kings Cross, where he could see the live game on SKY at Everton on the Sunday afternoon before catching the train home. As he sat in that familiar bar, scene of the previous row about Shearer and Geordie patriotism, and scene of the meeting with brother Dave years earlier for the Supermac hat trick against United, Brian noticed something very strange and worrying. The tv was showing some old goals and clips of Premiership clashes, with Beckham seeming to feature prominently, and it was ten minutes before the kick off against Everton at Goodison.

A quick enquiry led to panic, as they did not have the game on, and he ran off at full speed down the Caledonian Road. At least he thought he was on that road, but had taken the wrong turning, and could not find a bar, until he finally reached a seedy joint which seemed likely to do the business. It did so, except in another context, as it was an Egyptian dancers and strippers club, and the bemused bouncer told Brian that there was no football there, but he was welcome to meet the girls. He looked even more perplexed when the black and white clad character ran across the road and into a shortcut onto the Caledonian Road, where he found a Scottish pub with SKY, two minutes before kick-off.

Brian soon joined a group of exiled Mags. None of them had ever met, but after five minutes they were like brothers in arms. Robert scored, Graveson made a filthy tackle, and Mr Wayne Rooney helped the Blue Scousers win 2-1. A wild-looking Elswick lad had previously spoken to Brian of his anxiety over the prominent love bite on his neck – he had been up home for a few days, and was due back at his girlfriend's flat in West London. By the end of the match, his anxiety was displaced by dejection, and he muttered that he was off to stay with one of his mates instead. How many romances have been ruined by this club? Brian thought briefly of a few of his own, including the ill-fated two-week one with that Sunderland lass many years ago, and another one which collapsed after a United home defeat. It has to be said that the Elswick lad's relationship may already have been in serious bother anyway.

The strange season was not over yet. On April 12th, a week after this defeat, a far bigger one blasted in at St James, with the Mancs banging in six goals, and Newcastle getting two. Scotty and some of the others wandered, just wandered, down into the Quayside, and spent little time looking at the normally marvellous view or talking about the game. They were all in a state of shock. At the end of the month, they were back in town, where total panic was sweeping through groups desperately trying to find a location for the screening of the away derby at Sunderland.

Scotty and Brian soon realised that there would no televised coverage, allegedly on the instructions of the police who were probably tired of quelling disturbances, after live derby games, in Consett, Chester, Washington, and a host of other divided towns in the region. Rumours were everywhere, mobiles were in action, and one lad raced off to South Shields in the belief that the match was on in a dockland bar. This seemed unlikely, and even if it was, which was extremely unlikely, he did not seem to consider how he would be able to get inside that place with a Metro journey ahead of him. Half of Tyneside would already have been in there anyway by that time.

The ex-flatmates meanwhile settled for an afternoon in the Duke of Wellington just off the Bigg Market, watching the SKY results service. At one point, it seemed that Shearer had scored, which he had not. At another, total chaos broke out when a bloke jumped up with joy, and the rest all followed. Only his leap was due to the fact that his horse had just won him money at nearby

Ladbrokes, and he had to make a hasty departure over there after the false hope he had just caused. Nobby finally did the trick though, and the old enemy were beaten 1-0. Graham spent the early evening ringing bars in Sunderland asking if so and so was in – Shay, Alan, and others, only to have the phones slammed down on him when he gave the surnames: Given, Shearer, etc.

The 2003 season was over. Painfully, something else was also over, which naturally caused much angst and distress for Brian, Wendy, and the three children. The second marriage was finally over, and after a temporary stay with John in Heaton, Brian was in one of Kev's properties at the Marina down at the bottom of Byker, or St Peter's Basin as residents prefer to call it. John was a good bloke, a dedicated Aldershot fan, with an affiliation to Brighton, and a liking for the Mags, wisely accompanied by a cautious scepticism on the over-inflated claims of NUFC followers. His initial introduction to Geordie passion had taken place on a Metro, when the driver announced that United had just scored, and old grannies all shouted with joy. He was astonished. Once ensconced in the Marina, football talk was thin on the ground, although Aileen, who worked with Wendy, lived nearby, and was always ready to talk about life at St James.

By Christmas, Brian had his second meeting in London with Marion, herself a fanatic. As 2004 drifted on, she began to stay up in his rented flat more often. Later they moved into Heaton together, which gave much easier access to Brian's daughters. The move itself from her

Southern base managed to see Marion offend the removal men hired by Brian via an old school contact, as they were Mackems. As time passed by in Heaton, little Kirsty and little Becky were regularly wearing their strips and singing *Hey Alan Shearer, Oo, Ah, A Wanna Know How You Scored That Goal.* Work life was changing too, as it became clear that Joyce the MP was planning to retire in the 2005 election

The workplace itself was brilliant, as the office had previously moved to Design Works in Felling. The Toon crack was relentless, with Keith and Sue in the cafe. Keith in particular hated his job, and seemed to overcome the boredom behind the counter by talking about anything to do with Newcastle United. This suited Brian, who was noted for his long stays in that cafe, with one of his files alongside him, talking to Keith about anything to do with Newcastle United. Darren and Mark too were always ready to discuss United, as was Julie at the reception, although Brian made the sign of the cross whenever he had to go into her room. She was NUFC, but thought David Beckham was attractive and had his photo on her wall.

Round the corner in the Fox after work, there was always time for further crack with Kenny and Stewie, the former predicting glory, and the latter predicting disaster. Stewie, an alcohol and drugs counsellor, had managed to cure himself out of his black and white drug habit, or so he claimed – yet whenever a game was on the tv, his reactions did not quite confirm that he was over his addiction. Young Barry was around, on and off, and Malla, the Fox DJ, was another

fanatic. He had an anxious smile on his face
whenever they discussed a forthcoming fixture.
Finally, there was Eddie the Domino Man, who
turned out on a Friday tea-time, always sporting
his strip. He was one of the victims of the 90s
when less well-off fans were driven out of St
James, but he was as fanatical and dedicated as
ever. His domino game could easily be distracted
by some heated debate over the form, or lack of
it, of a player.

Before that 2003-4 season kicked off,
Brian was off to Oban to join the estranged
Wendy and the three girls. Sitting at the Central
Station one July Saturday, waiting for the
Edinburgh train and reading the Journal back
page, Brian noticed a very large group of dodgy-
looking characters. He quickly observed some
less dodgy-looking sporting Sunderland scarves,
and a quick glance at the friendly fixtures
confirmed that they were playing away inn
Edinburgh, against Hibs. This was not good news,
as he had to catch that train, or he would miss his
connections up to Oban. It was not good news
because he was wearing a Black & White top, and
any other dresswear was already in that Scottish
resort. Not that any change of clothes would have
helped, as his holiday clothes, like those of so
many Mags, normally consisted of enough NUFC
tops for each day, with perhaps one shirt for a
meal out.

Brian knew that the dodgy bunch were
Seaburn Casuals hooligan firm, the rivals of the
Newcastle Gremlins, and he phoned Scotty's
house to ask Tracey if she fancied a trip to
Edinburgh in order to protect him. They laughed

at his plight, and he boarded one of the longest train journeys of his life.

The Casuals were everywhere, and his interest in the Journal intensified, as occasional abuse and anti-Mag songs were hurled at him. He longed to be in the company of some of his mates, or better still, even the Gremlins. Potential disaster struck just south of Berwick, when Mother Nature forced him to run the gauntlet to the bog. One of them stuck his legs across the path to the toilet, and asked him for his shirt, adding that they would have fun burning it in Edinburgh. Brian refused, not because he was worried about travelling all the way up Loch Lomond without a top on, but because he was not giving his strip up for anybody, particularly to a SAFC thug. Threatened with a departure through the window, and probably to his death, Brian said a quick Jesus, Mary, and Joseph At least his passing would have taken place in the region.

The menacing character weighed up the situation, working out that being arrested at Berwick would spoil his day out. He shouted to his mates that there were bigger fish to fry than banging the Mag, as they had to smash Edinburgh up. As the moment passed, Brian smiled with relief, and with the knowledge that the Hibis, and the Jambos too, would not take kindly to such an attitude, and would ensure that those hooligans would not be able to implement their plan. He also, he has to admit, smiled on the following weekend when he returned to Heaton, to discover that the Newcastle Gremlins had met those characters after their return from the Hibs game.

By August, the real business, on the pitch and not off it, was under way. It began with a huge disappointment, when the club failed to get past Partisan Belgrade in a qualifier for the Champions League. There was no major title push that season. In December, Brian suddenly found important business to do in London, which strangely coincided with an away match as Charlton. He did some work at the Commons on the Thursday, and planned to go with Emily and her boyfriend, who worked in the London office, to a party in South London on the Friday night. Instead, by chance, he met Marion for the second time, stayed overnight at her remote house in Essex, and travelled down to the match with her and her son David. Both followed the Mags everwhere, to St James, and across Europe, so this trip was more of a home match for them in terms of miles.

Both Marion and David were, and still are, utter fanatics. Their 500-mile round trips to home games had certainly seen some incidents. On one occasion, they made it to the Tyne Bridge, only to turn straight round, and drive straight back south, having discovered a match against Southampton was off due to a snowstorm. On another, their car broke down at Durham, much to the amusement of a coach-load of Leeds fans. The car was towed into a garage and repaired at rapid speed. The pair had the last laugh when United defeated Leeds. Their European travels sometimes saw them with the United hard core in some remote country or with the thousands who made it to places like Barcelona and Milan. As the song goes: *Have You*

Ever Seen A Mackem In Milan?

Wisely, Marion had not taken her son to Belgrade. There, the Serbian police seemed on the verge of firing into a crowd of Mags, and they were all forced to retreat into the British Embassy. She knew some of Brian's mates, such as Ian, and Bryan with whom she had worked on the Fans Liaison Committee when she was the Chairman. Marion talked football at any opportunity and did so on that visit to Charlton. She would do so with Brian as a couple over the next three years. They may have had many arguments during those years together, but their love of NUFC was a strong bond, although it could lead to heated discussions on the ability of Shola Ameobi or indeed the future of the club.

That day in South London against Charlton, however, they separated and Brian caught up with Kev, joining Ian, Big Dave, Piper, and half the Toon Army, it seemed, amidst crazy but friendly scenes in a social club near the ground. It was a boring 0-0 draw on the pitch, but as usual, the away end rocked to the sound of the Geordie musical repertoire. As always, the now common ban on standing throughout the game was totally ignored, and the group left the ground afterwards for the local social club. Only this time, the large skinhead South London bouncers apologetically stated they could not allow them all inside, due to some general ban imposed by the Committee on away fans after the game. Geordies are natural rebels, and Ian decided on a new tactic, starting off a bout of Christmas carols amongst the frozen Mags. This racket continued, until the barman relented, on the agreement that if they would stop singing those bloody carols in his car park, he would let them in.

A couple of hours later, Kev and Brian were up at London Bridge in search of a pint before travelling over to his place in Ealing. They bumped into Piper again, and his endless knowledge and list of contacts meant that they joined him in one of the pubs around there, despite previous refusals of entry.

Chapter Twenty-eight

Another departure

In January 2004 it was FA Cup time again, and the new romance was blossoming, so the pair set off for Liverpool and Anfield. Arriving at Lime Street station, they noticed three angry Geordies shouting at a group of Scousers that if this was the City of Culture, then they were having a laugh. He foolishly booked a room in the Adelphi Hotel in the city, as he had previously known it as up-market – it was actually a former meeting place of Harold Wilson and Labour Government members back in another era. Only the hotel now seemed to have gone back in a different era, that of the old Eastern European Communist bloc. It resembled something out of downtown Leningrad, and the attitude of the staff seemed to fit this image perfectly.

Recovering from the lack of welcome, the couple took in the sights of the city on the Saturday morning, which passed a good half-hour, had a drink next to the Mersey, and caught a taxi up to Anfield. The driver was talkative and friendly, an Everton supporter, who insisted that they were the local team now, as Liverpool had a following fast resembling that of the Mancs.

Familiar scenes took place: Geordies fighting each other at the Arkle – deja vue – and a visit to a packed bar further down the road, where the Red Scousers resented the presence

and noise volume of their Geordie visitors.
Likewise in the ground, where history repeated
itself, with the Kop outsung, and United defeated,
this time, 2-1, despite a fantastic Robert goal.
Nearby Scousers taunted the Mags, and Brian lost
his degree, a phrase often used by Big Mark who
suggested any signs of his university education
collapsed when watching United. Marion was
perturbed by his state of mind after the match as
he looked menacingly at the mocking, boastful
Reds. They flagged down a bus, the driver, with
the inevitable moustache, laughed and told them
to cheer up and have a laugh, and then Marion
lost her degree on the journey back into the town.
They stayed in that hotel for the night, having no
intention of going out, and Marion went down
with a migraine.

The next morning, and in gloomy mood,
Brian went down to breakfast in search of toast
for his beloved, only to be told he was not
allowed to carry toast back to the room. He saw
some of the Azure Blue lads, and a brief chat
confirmed they were also in the same mood.
Marion was eventually able to get out of bed at
11.00am, and they ordered a cup of tea, which
never arrived. They caught the train back home
about 1.00pm, out of that bloody hotel, bloody
Liverpool, and of course, out of That Bloody FA
Cup.

The rest of the season was hardly a
disaster, as although Premiership glory was not on
the horizon, Bobby's team were still a top six side.
Marion, by now a true companion as well as a
fanatical Mag – a great combination! – wanted to
visit Dublin in St Paddy's week. This nearly led to

the couple missing a home game against Charlton
in March. It was an odd trip anyway, as both were
forced to stay in another Liverpool hotel before
travelling to Holyhead after the ferry was
cancelled. Marion's passion for Brian was sorely
tested in that forced stay in Liverpool. Brian's ego
just about survived. While they were indulging in
the hotel bedroom, Marion was occasionally
glancing at the Barca-Madrid match on the tv in
the background.

Worse was to come, as they were
stranded in Dublin on the Friday night due to the
conditions in the Irish Sea. The only option was a
plane, which was not brilliant news for Brian with
his panic disorder, and medication levels had to
be raised dramatically. They had to leave, as
United were playing Charlton on the Saturday.
They got to that match, and saw Shearer put two
goals in, along with that other bloke, Jenas.

Meanwhile, the UEFA Cup run continued
and took United into the semi-final against
Marseilles. The away tie was a disaster, as injuries,
and the talented French, knocked Newcastle out:
another chance for that trophy gone. Brian,
Marion, and all the rest had that familiar feeling of
loss and despair. By now there was a growing
view that Bobby had lost control of the likes of
Dyer and Bellamy, who have long since
deservedly been forgotten. The away match at
Liverpool in May was an important one, as fifth
place and the UEFA Cup were now the target, and
not the Champions League.

The night before the game, Kev boomed in on his
mobile from a tube in West London, slightly the
worse for wear, and made a defiant speech that

the Toon Army would never be defeated. He was
in rather loud voice, so God only knows what his
fellow passengers thought of him, as he sounded
like a Japanese kamikaze pilot. He declared that
he would never ever surrender, missed his stop,
and was left looking for a tube back to where he
actually lived. United did get a draw at Anfield,
watched by Marion and Brian in the Star back in
town, whilst Kev, Ian, and others, sang their songs
of defiance down in Liverpool. So did the packed
Star.

The summer of 2004 brought in players,
including the legendary Patrick Kluivert, who
soon proved that his legendary days and
dedication to football were well behind him. And
then came yet another dull August. Freddy
Shepherd sacked Bobby. History has since been
re-written by some Mags, as they forget that the
vast number were increasingly unhappy with
Robson. Nevertheless, the undignified sacking of
a man who bled Black & White, unlike some of
his players, was awful, as he should have at least
been offered some kind of title such as Director
of Football or Honorary Whatever.

Moreover, Freddy, just like he had done
with Dalglish, had managed to sack a manager in
August, just as the season started. Forward
planning again, and this time there was nobody
lined up for the hot or rather burning seat. An
embarrassing trawl took off, and at one point, it
seemed that only Scotty, Kev, and Ian had not
been approached for the job. Enter Graeme
Souness in September, the man who would bring
such committed stars such as Boumsong, Amdy
Faye, and Albert Luque, and his increasingly dour

side finished 14th in the 2004-5 season.

In late January, daughter Claire took her second Rite of Passage, with a trip to Arsenal and their Library, as it was known due to the lack of noise at Highbury. United lost, but she was hooked, loving the atmosphere and crack in the away end. Her Dad's panic disorder meant that he had to avoid any bus travel, and part of the rail track was down. This led to a train journey to Cambridge, and a very expensive taxi to Peterborough station to catch up with Ian, Terry, and Big Dave, who had reached there via a replacement bus.

On the ongoing train journey, Big Dave was far from impressed when some younger Mags made some kind of lewd comment about Claire and he let his feelings be known in no uncertain manner. Things began to deteriorate under Souness. It became the era when fans felt that they just had to turn up at St James out of duty, like some kind of dull, boring job, trapped in the ground by the already paid-for season tickets.

Yet that first season had actually promised glory, well away from the League, in Europe and in the FA Cup. The Mags clung on with growing hope and optimism. By March 2005, Mourinho's Chelsea were at Gallowgate for a Cup quarter-final, and faced a North East blizzard and a blistering, raucous atmosphere. The Special One used his three subs, only for Big Al to flatten one of their other players, and reduce them to ten men. The ground rocked once again, and a Cup semi-final was on the agenda.

The European drive was running parallel, and on the Friday before Aston Villa at home, and the European tie against Sporting Lisbon, Shearer announced that he was staying on for another year. This news was swept off the front and back pages within 24 hours, as Bowyer and Dyer fought each other at St James in front of 50-odd thousand disgusted supporters. This was far from ideal preparation for the Cup game in Portugal and for the semi-final in Cardiff against the Mancs.

NUFC then entered into another one of those weeks which broke hearts and spirits. The team simply never turned up in Lisbon, and crashed out of the UEFA Cup. And they certainly never turned up in Cardiff for another reunion with Sir Alex and the FA Cup semi-final against the Mancs. Claire, Brian, and Marion stayed in a hotel for the weekend, and bought some t-shirts, printed with the words "We Never Win Fuck All." This was perhaps a reflection, or subconscious preparation, for the Sunday contest with the Mancs. They wandered around Cardiff on the Saturday, and watched Arsenal on the tv as they strolled into the final.

Afterwards, the Gooners approached Dad and daughter – Marion was going down with a migraine – and offered them all the best for the Sunday match, but neither were fooled that they had suddenly developed a love for the Toon Army. They just wanted to make sure that they were playing Newcastle and not Manchester United in the final. To the bafflement of the pair, the Arsenal fans were not jumping into lakes, or climbing walls in celebration of a semi victory. They just seemed to see it as a normal day at the office for them, which it was of course.

Sunday, and yes, a normal day at the

office for the NUFC nation, now swamping the
Welsh capital in their thousands. Gus and his son
young Andy, who was creating a good reputation
for accurate betting on football, landed at the
hotel after the marathon bus journey from
Newcastle, along with other recognisable faces.
Before that fixture, some Man U fans complained
that they had so far to travel, and the game should
have been played at Leeds or somewhere. This
missed two points. Their London, Cornish, or
whatever followers would have had to make a far
longer journey up to Yorkshire, and a massive
ground was needed to accommodate the demand
for tickets on Tyneside. Soon the hotel was
packed, as news spread that the bar was open,
and startled tourist guests encountered the Toon
Army hordes. It quickly turned into a kind of old
Leazes End by 10.30am.

Then it was off to the stadium via a pub.
There was little sight of the opposition, apart from
outside one place, where they tried to mock the
group, only for the Fuck All Shirts to be lifted up
from underneath the Black & White tops. This
stunned them and they shut up, and for the rest
of the day, Cardiff belonged to the Geordies, apart
from on the pitch itself of course. The team were
an absolute disgrace, and Nicky Butt was a
particular target of abuse when they trooped off
at the end. There was a view that he had been
Ferguson's twelfth man, but it was later
discovered that Nicky was actually carrying an
injury, and would be finally welcomed back into
the fold in the distant future.

Whilst the performance was pathetic, the
noise and support from the NUFC was not, and

echoed around the ground: *4-1 And You Still Can't Sing*. Ian, Brian, Fred, Nick, Claire, and all the rest sang their hearts out. So did John, a Gateshead councillor and famous for his anti-Mackem jokes, who sadly left for Another Place a year later, without seeing that elusive trophy. The group actually hit the front page of the Journal on the Monday, with a photo of their section singing their heads off at the end of the match in defiance. It was blown up by Ian, and is on the walls of some of them.

Chapter Twenty-nine

The Road to Wigan Pier

Not quite a homecoming this time, but a new arrival landed in town. This took Claire and Brian to St James along with 20,000 others, to welcome him. Michael Owen had been signed, and it was time for wild, crazy scenes again. This was a new idol, who would play alongside the Lion of Gosforth. Unlike the Shearer Homecoming, Felling Kenny and Stewie were not there, but they weren't missed as pictures of Geordie fanaticism boomed across global tv. The SKY presenter, who did seem taken aback by the atmosphere, asked the welcoming party to sing their favourite song. It was not the Blaydon Races. *We Are The Geordies, The Geordie Boot Boys, And We Are Mental And We Are Mad, By Far The Loyalist Football Supporters, The World Has Ever Had,* echoed around the old Leazes.

Brian told his young daughter, dressed in full regalia, that this was the biggest news to hit town for almost a decade. Little did the fanatical gathering know that Owen was only to play thirteen games by the end of the 2006-7 season, and that speculation would mount that he would leave even before the 2007-8 season even started.

The 2005-6 season stumbled on. Owen played some games at least - some. And then came the scent of glory. Marion and Brian had planned a romantic autumn weekend in Paris but chose Wigan instead for a vital Carling Cup tie. The Carling Cup would do for United fans, and the 6.000 ticket allocation meant that they outnumbered the home crowd by 1,000. Optimism turned to euphoria when they learnt that Wigan were going to field a team with only one first team regular in it. Some joy took place in the hotel bedroom with Marion long before the match, but this was to be the only pleasure to be had that day. They met up with familiar faces, Paul and Mick, the brothers of Fr Steve, various old characters from distant years, and of course, Ian. Marion went off in search of her ticket which she duly got from Bryan from Washington.

Once again it was time for the side not to turn up when it really, really mattered, and Wigan Reserves proceeded to pound the visitors and knock them out of the Cup. The huge away following tried to lift the players, but failed, and by the end of the match, were demanding the head of Souness, and trying to attack Freddy Shepherd's car. The next morning over breakfast in the gloomy hotel in Wigan, Marion pointed out the view to Brian: a bloody graveyard!

Wigan was the graveyard for Souness too, although it took a few more weeks before his burial, or rather sacking. He walked off with a healthy pay-off and with no invitation to come back to Geordieland for a drink. To be fair, Shepherd listened to the fans who increasingly demanded that Glenn Roeder be appointed after his early healthy stewardship of the rudderless ship. Suddenly, life became more rosy at St James again after the period of gloom and apathy. Relegation talk was soon dispelled, and the team

Wigan defeat proves graveyard for United & Souness

climbed the league at astonishing speed.

One match stands out: the public humilation inflicted upon Jermaine Jenas, as Spurs were demolished 3-1. He had left for London, noting that life in Newcastle was like living in a Goldfish Bowl, seemingly unaware that the players belong, or should belong, to the fans, and some pros accepted that fact as part of the passionate package. Jenas missed a sitter at the Gallowgate, and the place collapsed into chaos, as if the home side had scored. He left the field dejectedly, to sounds of *3-1 To the Goldfish Bowl*. He had received the usual treatment reserved for traitors, albeit without the missiles of previous decades. As Ginola once said, if you leave the Zebras under a cloud, you are never forgiven. If you leave as a hero, like Sir Les, you are welcomed back with open arms, at least until kick-off time.

There was one blip for Claire as United surged up the League. She now had a season ticket, bought by her Dad. This was bought as part of her education allowance package, something which did not quite convince her Mam Jane, who thought in terms of money for her studies. Marion arranged for Claire's birthday greetings to be read out on the tannoy at half time against, who else, Liverpool. Her Washington mates heard the bloke say "Congratulations to the 16-year old and for a decade following Newcastle." The opponents spoilt the day slightly by winning. Claire took it in her stride. By now she was a seasoned observer, and usually berated her Dad if he predicted that a goal was imminent or that so and so was playing well. She was often right, as he was so often proved wrong, usually within minutes.

Good times were coming back though, and Roeder remarkably took the side to seventh place and qualification for the Inter-Toto Cup, the competition which leads to the UEFA Cup, and seems to involve a season playing 80 games in Europe. Souness was history, and the club had somehow stumbled onto the continent again.

Before the season ended, Gus, Andy, Marion, and Claire took off for the Stadium of Light, but Brian's panic disorder meant that he was not able to travel. If ever proof that illness was needed by the DWP, then that was it. A huge convoy took off, as the SAFC had not sold all their tickets, and thus the Mag allocation was larger than usual. One Mag had spent the previous evening changing all the road signs to their ground, and the directions were now to the Stadium of Shite. He must have had some left over, as the National Glass Centre became the National Shite Centre. Brian was well represented that day by his daughter, who was under the so-called watchful eye of Gus. The SAFC had not won at home all season, scored, sang *Shearer, Shearer, What's The Score?* and six minutes later, Gus, Marion, all of them, sang the same song. United had gone 3-1 up and the Mags all witnessed Big Al score his last ever League goal, and make his last Premiership appearance, before he was carried off injured.

One lad told Gus that the six-minute flurry of NUFC goals were better than any six minutes he had ever spent in bed with a woman. Gus understood his reaction. The game finished 4-1, sweet revenge for that derby defeat against Sunderland by the same score at Gallowgate all those years ago. Claire, meanwhile, alongside Andy, carried off a small piece of red seat, which remains on her bedroom wall. Andy's is under his bed.

One very vital piece of business had to be completed at the end of that crazy season. Everybody wanted to be part of it, with the exception of Craig Bellamy who did not have an invite. He had long since said goodbye, but this was no bitter farewell. It was Time To Say Goodbye to the sheetmetalworker's son from Gosforth, standard-bearer of the flag, and the man who had shattered Jackie Milburn's goals record. The Shearer testimonial took place at an emotional, packed Gallowgate in a friendly against Celtic, against a cauldron of noise and sound which could be heard across the city. A fabulous female opera singer halted that volume within seconds, when she sang *Time To Say Goodbye.*

Big, tattood Geordie skinheads were silenced, with tears in their eyes. Shearer appeared again to take a penalty against the Celts, and scored. Brian's trouser-button broke, and he held up his pants with the free scarves given out for the game.

The Glasgow behaved themselves, enjoyed the occasion, and only caused a stir when they sang *You'll Never Walk Alone,* which was heartily booed by the Geordies. Wrong time, and wrong song, for such an occasion, and anyway, they have far better songs than that. One Celtic fan later told Brian that the Shearer penalty was unjustified, which it was, but he didn't really mean it. As the tears emerged that night, they reflected more than the retirement of the Local Hero. They reflected the end of his playing dedication to NUFC, his inability to get that elusive medal, and yet another decade without a trophy with the football club so loved in the city. Shearer was, well, just Shearer. Astonishingly, certain characters had resented Big Al at one point, and they were not SAFC either.

A few years earlier, Young Barry in Felling, some members of the group in the Irish Centre, and quite a few more in the ground had reckoned that he was finished. As is typical amongst Mags, this has subsequently been denied by the parties involved - erased from memories and the history books. One does have the courage to admit that he held this view, namely

Ian. Naturally, Brian and Scotty reminded him of his anti-Shearer days, as for once, they were both right about something. Shearer proved that as he smashed that Jackie Milburn goal-scoring record.

The memories are simply too many to recall, and every Mag has their own special one: the glorious shot against Everton; the semi finals; goal 201 against Portsmouth when he broke Wor Jackie's record. Robson Green, himself a devotee, heard that roar four miles away while he was filming for some production; and even Shearer's last-ever League goal at the Stadium of Shite. With his professionalism, devotion, and dedication to the Geordie nation, exemplified by the occasional appearance with a bandaged head, Shearer was the leader of more than a football club. He was the standard-bearer of a cause which dominated so many people's lives. He was gone, but never, ever, to be forgotten - just like Wor Jackie.

Life after Big Al saw the Roeder revival hit the rocks, and witness some dreadful football. Brian's own life hit some heavy rocks too. In this period, he was running into further difficulties, with his panic disorder and alcohol abuse finally catching up with him, big style. In November, he was in a hospital in York, and on the night before, prepared for his entry by watching a shock away victory in the UEFA Cup against Palermo. During his stay in hospital, Brian managed to confuse the staff when he ventured out on his own for the first time, facing panic attacks and avoiding alcohol. He watched a dull draw in a pub against Manchester City over an orange juice. This led to a concerned chat with his main nurse on the Monday morning. She had been worried about his panic disorder, as she knew he was out at the weekend, and she asked him how things had gone. He replied that it had not gone too well. He thought she was talking about the match.

Europe was the only bright spot on a rather gloomy horizon for the club. There were some dreadful league games, too many to mention. A home match against Bolton was a particularly miserable day out, and the night turned out to be worse, when some rather nasty new neighbours decided to hold one of their infamous parties. Brian was not amused, and having asked them politely to turn the racket down, later returned to their front door, only for an altercation to break out. Marion appeared, managed to find herself in the middle of the fracas, and her jaw was badly bruised. The very early hours of the morning were spent up at the General Hospital. Brian was threatened some days later, but when he replied that he would let a couple of people know that if something happened to him in a dark back alley, those friends would know who had been involved. Nothing ever did happen.

Christmas time saw home games and reunion time, with current faces, and characters from the past congregating in the Irish Centre watching Newcastle play Reading and Spurs: Fr Steve, Gus, Kev, Marion, Claire, Ian, Piper, and all the others. Out of the blue, Geordie re-appeared, having disappeared so many years ago. He had always had an inclination towards Celtic, and confirmed that he occasionally travelled up to watch them in Glasgow, but added that the Toon were still his true love. He was accompanied by a lad from Frankfurt, the boyfriend of his daughter. This immediately brought some friendly attention from Ian, who had been out to that city for the UEFA game.

Brother Dave made a rare appearance. On his return from the South years before, he had been generally frozen out of the ground due to financial costs. And Brian had also arranged to meet Ged from university days and writer of "Fifty Years of Hurt". The trouble was that nearly thirty years of hurt is a long time. They failed to make contact, not recognising each other and unable to find space in which to examine faces at close range. The Irish Centre before and after the match is no place for a casual wander.

In January it was time for another "Week That Woz" headline. The FA Cup was due in town, against the plastic Geordie Manc Bruce's Birmingham City, now in the Coca-Cola Championship league or whatever its name was that year. The little matter of an away match at Spurs was shown live on the Sunday, and should have given some early warning signs. Due to an injury list the length of the Tyne, and the lack of a transfer policy the previous summer, the young United team were bombarded at White Hart Lane. Their average age seemed to about 13, and somehow they escaped with a win, as fancy, flowery Tottenham missed about 69 chances. It was a warning, unheeded of course.

The Cup run was ready for its launch on the Wednesday, and Brian put a fiver on for United to lift the Cup, thus proving that he had not read the runes, again. Another and far more ominous sign after that Spurs game was conveniently ignored, namely that the game was to be shown live on BBC national tv. The Chronicle covered a statement from Freddy Shepherd, proclaiming how very proud he was of the performances of his young boys who had been forced to plug a horrendous injury list, which must have seen a very full club doctor's surgery every Monday morning. None of that sick note group could compare though to the infamous Marcelino of previous years, who managed to get signed off for weeks with a bad finger.

On that back page against Bruce's Brummies that Wednesday, the Chronicle led with Freddy's statement that the youngsters played with pride and were a joy to watch. The Punters' Panel, in the same paper and in the Journal, all predicted an easy victory. Their views and wide-ranging emotions are certainly an accurate reflection of the NUFC tribe. On this occasion, they simply confirmed the mood of their fellow Mags.

Their mood, and that of their Black & White comrades, was very different by 10.00pm that night. Millions switched on to witness a humiliating 5-1 slaughter at Gallowgate, and the destruction of that young side. The traditional public apology was issued on the Thursday, this time from the manager. This was soon displaced by alarming news that the Turkish midfielder, Emre, had allegedly been involved in a racist incident against some Everton players in a previous fixture, and the national press was at it again. This race row caused more concern in town than the one which was going on inside the

Big Brother series, and had caused the Chancellor to apologise to the Indian sub-continent. Friday's news then switched to the future of the club, when it was confirmed that would-be new owners were not going to buy it. With no big investment on the horizon, Freddy was going nowhere.

Fans were not in a good mood. Brian was naturally in a similar frame of mind as he caught a bus down Shields Road in Byker. He noticed that one bookie's shop had forgotten to take down the massive sign from the window still emblazoned with the words "FA Cup Fever." Captain Scotty Parker managed to darken the mood further by calling on the fans to "get behind the team" for the Saturday league fixture against West Ham. Parker was clearly no expert on the history of Newcastle United Football Club. If he had been, he would have stated that the team would try and get behind the fans. A dull, dour draw should have ended the week, but tradition is all at St James. The Sunday Sun front page led with Freddy launching a blistering attack on John Hall, thus rounding off matters with a good old internal row. Scotty, Brian, and the rest, spent time arguing who hated the club the most, and meant it.

As the league performances deteriorated, one bright star remained in the North East sky, and once again, optimism soon pushed pessimism aside with the push towards the UEFA Cup final. Having scrapped their way through the Inter-Toto, and through the endless group stages of the competition, United were moving onto the big stage. Some of the group had made the journey with them. Ian had made it to Frankfurt, against the background of a worrying operation, although he told Brian that he had been going to Germany anyway. Gus emerged to claim that he was one of the few people to have actually seen the Inter-Toto Cup, somewhere in Spain in Valencia. He had previously toured their stadium with young Andy, dressed in Black & White strip.

Andy & Gus spot Inter-Toto Cup in Valencia's trophy cabinet

As the guide showed the tour party Valencia's major trophies, including the UEFA Cup, the pair had run out of the queue, much to the bewilderment of the guide and the rest of the tour. Andy had spotted the Inter-Toto Cup. Few Mags actually believed it existed. The latest version of that Cup was to appear at St James. Apparently, Newcastle had won it, although none of the group wanted to win the lottery which would let a fan stand next to it on the pitch. They still had some pride after all.

As these final stages of the UEFA loomed, talk turned to plans for the biggest party which would ever take place. It would be at the Final in Glasgow in May, when the entire Geordie nation could decamp for a few days and grab that trophy. Hurdles had to be overcome naturally. One was in Ghent against Wareghem. Their ground was deemed too small, and hence the fixture was held in that quaint Belgian medieval town. Marion discovered a low-cost package via the Eurostar with two nights in a hotel there, but a job interview meant that she was replaced by Kenny from Felling days.

Ghent was full of Mags, many in search of tickets, and there were various scenes of drunkenness and debauchery. There was no violence, as the Feyenoord boys had decided not to visit the Geordies this time. The town was beautiful, but many spent most of their time indoors. At the hotel itself, the perplexed manager asked Kenny and Brian if one group knew that the buckets of Belgian beer that they were drinking were powerful in alcohol content. He pointed out that it was only 11.00am on the day of the match. Kenny confirmed that the group would know the potential impact of the buckets. Sure enough, one of them missed the game, slept on a couch, and woke up to hear details of the match from his mates.

The details included news of a victory, albeit not a brilliant one. The atmosphere in the United end was bouncing and electric. Ian, famous for his whistling, was out-whistled, which in itself was a rare occasion. *Phillippe – Phillippe, Phillippe Albert, Everybody Knows His Name* - was spotted in the seats as that song echoed around the stadium. It was accompanied by another song: *Tell All the Friends Ya Know, United Are Going To Glasgow, Been To Italy, And Germany, And Now We're Going To Glasgow.* Post-match was a bit of a disaster for Kenny and Brian, as they were going in the opposite direction to most of the Mags, ready to be bussed by the heavy Belgian policing operation to the airport or train station.

They soon climbed over a wall, and onto the main road back into town, roughly the distance between Low Fell and the town back home. The police told them all public transport, including taxis, was banned from the area, and that they would have to walk back. Trudging along that road, they eventually hailed a taxi-driver, who was hovering just inside the transport ban area. He took them back into town, which unfortunately was closed, probably on the order of the police.

The pair caught their pre-booked taxi from the hotel at 5.20am the next morning, to make the vital connection for the only Eurostar that they could board on their cheap travel deal. Brian felt chilly and decided to put his long overcoat over his jacket, only to realise that he had left it in the foyer. He had a simple choice: return to the hotel, miss the train, and pay a fortune for another Eurostar, or leave the coat and mobile where they were. It was no choice really. There was more to come. They arrived in London early morning, had a couple of pints near

Trafalgar Square, and set off up to Kings Cross to catch the pre-booked cheap return back home at 3.00pm. They found the station in utter chaos, as some major problem further up the line led to news that there would be no further trains going up North that day.

Some headed off to Euston to try and get to Manchester or Carlisle, while others hung around aimlessly. Brian decided to have a quiet word with a driver in uniform. He turned out to be a Geordie, and quietly told him that there was no way he was not getting home that night. The driver's contacts had told him that a train would be put on at 8.00pm that night, but the station was not taking the risk of informing the masses.

Brian, and some of the other Mags, opted for a few hours around the corner in a Caledonian Road pub, while Kenny and some others heard of some train heading over to East Anglia and a bus trip back to some other train, and chose this option. As that 8.00pm train pulled into Peterborough an hour or so after leaving Kings Cross – the driver was right, of course – Brian, sitting with a bunch of Durham NUFC in the crowded train – saw a harrassed and knackered-looking Kenny climb on board. He had spent hours travelling around East Anglia, and he somehow did not see the funny side when Brian shouted his greetings.

The complications of the journey mattered little, as the song boomed out again all the way back to the region: *Tell All the Friends Ya Know, United Are Going To Glasgow.* Only they weren't. The next opposition were the tough, and high scoring Dutch outfit, AZ Alkmaar. Ian and others were already making plans for the final in Scotland, and when United thrashed AZ at St James in the first leg, they seemed right. Four goals rained in. The Dutch managed to get two back, but the task ahead seemed relatively straightforward. Just be cautious and tight, and get that away goal or even two in the return leg. This strategy omitted two important factors – namely that Roeder was about to get the tactics wrong, and, far more important, Newcastle United have a reputation for not turning up on the big occasion, with few noteable exceptions. The team showed no passion, no commitment, nothing, and the trip to Glasgow was off.

Brian's own life was not exactly back on course, as he watched this game back in that York hospital. He was again being treated for alcohol abuse and panic disorder, and it was finally confirmed that he suffered from a form of PTSD. This later led to an evening stay as a guest with Northumbria police at Market Street. This was after a flair-up relating to Marion's connections with a Scottish bloke, and Brian sampled those coppers' fine, caring accommodation. Knowing of his panic disorder, they refused to allow him his medication as they held him, without charge, in a tiny cell. This same period later led him to a stay in the RVI after a failed suicide attempt. Thankfully, it failed and taught him never to take such a route again, above all for his beloved daughters.

Back in that York hospital, anticipating a decent result in Alkmaar, he had watched the game with Dave, a decent Huddersfield Town fan, and the latter could not believe what he was seeing. Brian could, and at the end of the match he stormed out of the lounge, managing to miss Marion's David on screen sticking the V-sign up at Roeder in front of millions of viewers, including some of his former teachers back in Essex. Meanwhile, Brian's rapid exit from that room caused some consternation with the staff, as rumour spread that he had had another attack. Only the Huddersfield fan knew the real cause of his reaction, and that it was not related to post-trauma. Well, not in one sense anyway.

The rest of his stay in York saw some telephone contact from his Mag circle, and yet again, arguments about who hated the club the most. Graham sent a particularly sensitive message, in which he stated that if the hospital resident ever thought that the Mags would win anything, then the treatment was simply not working. For perhaps the only time in their lives, Scotty, Brian, Marion, Graham, and some of the others, actually wanted United to lose their league match at Charlton on the Sunday. A heroic triumph would have been too much to bear. These debates, of course, totally baffled the Huddersfield supporter. Roeder himself was now finished, and it was only a matter of time. The university-trained manager had sadly been found out, although his bad luck with injuries has to be remembered as partly a cause of his downfall. He had finally lost the fans. Alkmaar was yet another kick in the proverbials. For some of the older generation, it seemed to be the final straw.

The story was far from over - it never is. Ian had previously applied for a set of UEFA Cup Final tickets via a website, and was successful.

They arrived through his letterbox two days after the Dutch disaster. Meanwhile, Gus was out in Alicante, inspecting his newly-bought property. He had left the pub as United disintegrated on the TV screen, and sought out a quiet bar without any TV at all. Half an hour later, the one and only Alkmaar fan in the area stormed in, and collected his winnings from the Spanish barman on a bet he had placed. The next morning, Gus ordered a taxi to the airport, only to cancel it. The driver was that only Alkmaar fan in the area.

UEFA Cup Final tickets arrive two days after United crash out

Kev, meanwhile, was stuck up a mountain somewhere in Chile, clearly the best place to be. Fr Steve texted Brian, stating he was in a state of despair. Where was his faith when he needed it? thought Brian.

Chapter Thirty

From Disastrous to Ridiculous

And then it was time for the absurd. The club, with perfect timing, launched a new strip. It was advertised with huge billboards of Michael Owen, despite the fact that he had rarely been sighted by fans on the pitch since he signed. Freddy also spoke of making the stadium even bigger to accommodate all the fans. Along with the obvious insensitivity in timing, it coincided with news that Niall Quinn, the Sunderland chairman, had stayed with some of their fans at an airport in Bristol after they had been unjustly thrown off a plane for singing. He paid for their taxis back to Wearside. This contrasted badly with the fortunes of Marion's son David, and Bryan, who had been forced to wander the streets in search of taxis in Alkmaar after the club had failed to provide enough buses to get back to Amsterdam.

For some inexplicable reason, Brian decided to visit the club museum, which just about sums up life with United. True, there's the Fairs Cup photos, and much glorious history, well, from a previous century at least. There's Wor Jackie, Hughie Gallagher, Shearer and the rest. But really, the Texaco Cup, the Anglo-Italian Cup, Terry McDermott's medals (with Liverpool and England), and the daft plaque about the Premiership's best ever match (which, to remind you, Newcastle lost). That museum simply does not compare to the memorabilia to be seen in the Strawberry or the Adelphi.

Gus then decided to present Brian with a clipping he had discovered about the motto of Newcastle United, taken from the days of good King Charles. He had seen a poster of it opposite a new bus station in town, and it confirmed that the club had salvaged the Newcastle coat of arms. "Fortifer Defendit Triumphans" – Triumphing through a Brave Defence. The castles had been replaced with Black & White stripes. Given that United were not exactly renowned for a strong defence, under Keegan and, far worse, with the likes of Titus Bramble and his cohorts, Gus was clearly in a sarcastic mood.

"Triumphing through a brave defence" Fans flabergasted by English version

As if this was not enough, the Alkmaar disaster that is, not Gus's motto presentation, the league position was about to become increasingly dangerous. Back in January, after the Birmingham FA Cup fiasco and Captain Scotty's misplaced rallying call to the Toon Army, that home game against the Hammers witnessed a pathetic opening: two sloppy goals, a crap defender injured, a disputed NUFC goal, and an equalizer.

As the league results declined, and with it the standard of football, that haunting word appeared: relegation. It was only a possibility, but the team began to flirt with it, and if they carried on until the end of the season in that fashion, it could well have happened. Brian, armed with his medication, managed to travel down to Sheffield United. As a means of staving off his panic disorder, he booked into an hotel the night before the game. United needed a result there, or flirtation was in danger of becoming consummation. Brian found himself in the middle of a Northern Ireland Reconciliation Trip, and met up with the mixed victims and participants of the Troubles, thankfully at an end. He chatted with Frankie from West Belfast, and on the Saturday morning they had a pint together before Brian was due to meet up with Ian, Terry, Big Dave, and the rest from the Irish Centre.

The potential danger of relegation seemed to have brought down some of the old Geordie tribes not renowned for wearing suits and sitting in corporate boxes, not that most of the normal away following were like that anyway. Brian recognised some of the characters, as he looked out of the window in a quiet pub next to the hotel, only to see South Yorkshire police vans and horses everywhere. He popped out to buy some cigarettes, and noticed that the pub opposite was now surrounded by the local law enforcers. Inside it, the Mags were hanging out of windows and milling at the front door, waiting for the charge. The fact that they were singing *Harry Roberts is Our Friend, He Kills Coppers,* was clearly not easing the tension. Brian rejoined Frankie, who was now beginning to feel that he was back in West Belfast in the bad old days, and within minutes, mayhem broke out. One of the Mags, who had been at the door singing at the cavalry, managed to crawl through the melee, crossed the road into the quiet pub, saw Brian's Black & White strip, and muttered something about police harassment.

Leaving Frankie behind half an hour later, it was time to get up to Bramall Lane. The necessary result was achieved, and Terry hurled Brian down the terraces in delight. Back home, he returned to his flat and discovered that, despite a double-check in the hotel bedroom, he had left his set of keys behind. Marion was in Scotland, and the only other spare set was with her son David, who was down South. The result was a night at Scotty's, and a costly bill on the Sunday to replace the locks. Relegation was off the agenda, that was the main thing, and it was simply a case of waiting for the season to fizzle out. Instead, it exploded, all the way into the summer.

Matches still had to be attended. Graham and his Winlaton group had long since arranged a cheap hotel deal in the South to take in the

Reading game away. The game was moved, but they took in their weekend, and one of them pointed out that it was even better, as it meant that they did not have to go to that match and could just have a good time anyway. Graham agreed. Meanwhile, Brian missed the Chelsea home match, as he was staying with friends up a Spanish mountain in a bid to recover his health and sort out his life. There was little sign that he had learnt anything since that home game against Bedford Town in the early 60s. The road from Carlos's cottage was blocked by a mud deluge, so a lift into a nearby town to watch the game was out of the question. He actually asked his Spanish mate how far it was to the nearest village which might show the game, was told that it would be about an hour's walk, and seriously considered it for a while. The fact that he did not make the walk, albeit with some reluctance, perhaps meant that he had at least learnt something after all.

The last home game was Blackburn Rovers. By half-time, a very large and red-faced skinhead was demanding that one of the stewards downstairs at the Leazes End corner show him the exit door. He shouted that he wanted out of this hellhole, was never gannin' back, and asked the steward to pass on the message to Freddy and the Board. He will be back, and probably is by now. Bizarrely, at the end of the match, the announcer asked fans to remain seated to give the team a round of applause as they walked around the pitch. The few thousand who remained in the crowd did not know whether to boo or cheer, so did both. The noise outside the Directors' Box was louder, as the demonstrators shouted abuse.

They wanted Freddy out, and they wanted Roeder out. Their latter wish was soon granted. Another victim of life next to the old hanging-site.

Grim Reality Show – "I'm a Newcastle fan, get me out of here!"

One national paper alleged that some of the players were threatened in a nightclub on the Gateshead side of the river on the night after the Blackburn home game, having had the gall to show their faces. The 2006-7 season rounded off at Watford, where Obafemi Martens managed not to travel, and Nzogbia left the ground in the huff.

By this stage of the season, Watford was a total irrelevance for all Mags. Rarly, Marion and Brian were not even listening to the game, although the radio was on. She was selling her flat, and he was about to move again – to another part of Heaton – again. Another Brian, an old

Leazes-Ender, helped the shift some days later. Peter did as well, at one point, noted the split for a minute, said he was busy, and stayed for another hour to talk – about NUFC

Events off the pitch were taking over the NorthEastEnders Show. Freddy clashed with Michael Owen. Following talk of him lining up a move via a get-out clause, Freddy demanded that Owen make an official pledge of loyalty to United after almost two years of treatment for serious injuries. No pledge was forthcoming, and the situation turned into a farce when a couple of plastic Scousers – from Scarborough or somewhere – managed to trap Freddy on video camera, offering to carry Michael down to Liverpool for them. Often the laughing stock of the tabloids, it seemed never-ending, only the fans did not see the funny side.

Freddy sacked Roeder, or he resigned, and he had got his man by that Watford game: Big Sam Allardyce. The reaction was mixed, as Allardice had previously turned down United before Souness landed. Astonishingly, Big Sam was now the 19th manager in 52 years, and more astonishingly, the seventh in ten seasons. Also, Sam was the first newly-appointed manager since Gordon Lee in 1975 to actually take charge of the club with a full summer ahead and with time to prepare for a new season.

And it was still not over. The fans' reaction to the appointment of Big Sam was mixed. Graham did one of his famous somersaults, and predicted the dawn of New Era Number 33. Others were more lukewarm, whilst Marion was very hostile as was brother Dave. Ian,

Claire, and Fr Steve wanted to just wait and see. Before Sam had time to sit down properly in The Very Boiling Hot Seat, the Halls said goodbye to Freddy, who was stuck in hospital, and they sold out to Mike Ashley. The billionaire was said to be a recluse, but he would later been seen at matches wearing a Black & White top and jumping up and down like all the rest of the tribe, and going into Toon nightclubs wearing the said strip. He was actually stopped from getting into one, until one of the senior staff intervened to say that owners of a football club could wear a strip and get in.

Postscript

The story of Newcastle United could not be
invented. Nobody would believe it. And nobody
would believe that throughout all these years on
the Black & White rollercoaster, with some
wonderful highs and far more gut-wrenching
lows, the fans were, and still are, with their club,
despite moments when separation or even
divorce seems inevitable. The characters in this
book are simply a few amongst the so many who
follow this club with passion, devotion, and blind
loyalty, and, above all, with hope.

It is the culture, as daughter Claire's
MySpace states when asked about interests.
Culture, not an interest, she proclaims. Those fans
are United. They keep their Faith in song: *We Are
The Geordies, The Geordie Boot Boys, We Are
Mental And We Are Mad, By Far The Loyalist
Football Supporters, The World Has Ever Had*. And
they all want to be in that number, When the
Mags Go Marching In. If any future chairman or
manager can march them in, then their statues
will join those of Wor Jackie and the one prepared
for Big Al, and good luck to them. As Sir Alex
said, these fans deserve better, and Brian,
amongst all the others, hopes that they will get
their reward one day.

This work is a tribute to the fans who
make NUFC a big club. One day, perhaps, they
shall overcome, as the Leazes used to sing in the
1970s. Over to the chairman and the manager,
whomsoever they may be, with very, very best

wishes for the future. Some fans never give up, even just to look at the results, they never lose the bug. Most stay with the Lads, even if they have their sabbaticals and boycotts. It is, as Claire says, her culture, and that of so many others. This book is no detailed set of statistics. Others have done that much better, and some facts in this book are probably wrong. It matters little. This is just a reflection of a Black & White life and some of the oh so dedicated people in it. Gender, race, job status, money: nobody cares. They are simply Mags.

Keep the faith, as they say: *We Want To Be In That Number, When The Mags Go Marching In*.

Thanks

This work could not have been written without use of the sources of information available on the subject of Newcastle United. They are simply too many to mention, but special thanks are due to NUFC.com, the website of Biffa and Niall, fanzine writers such as Mick Edmondson and Mark Jensen (co-owners of the Back Page Bookshop), and historians such as Paul Joannou. Apologies for any inaccuracies, which will be mine and not theirs.

Obviously, this book could not have been appeared either without the many characters in it, or the thousands who are not. Some have helped, and special thanks are owed to them, especially Gus and a small circle of friends. Gratitude is also due to Chris, my extremely patient editor & publisher, for his help and guidance, and to our artist Paul Burke who produced a terrific series of cartoons at very short notice. A note of thanks is also due to my GP, who has helped me with the panic disorder which emerged in my later life.

Above all, this book is dedicated to all the followers of NUFC, and alongside them, to Mam, and three special young daughters, Claire, Kirsty and Becky.

Brian Hall
Heaton, Newcastle upon Tyne
December 2007

Author

Brian Hall was born in 1957 in a council house in Penshaw, County Durham, close to the pit community of Shiney Row. This was two years after Newcastle United completed their hat-trick of FA Cup Final victories, ie two years after they last won a major domestic trophy. Brian has lived most of his life in the North East, apart from periods in Liverpool, London and Luxembourg. His first job, while still at school, was selling the Football Pink. Since university, Brian has had various jobs, including elderly care, but most of his working life has been in politics and advice work.

Brian has supported Newcastle United from a very early age. Like so many thousands upon thousands of other supporters, he has experienced the highs and the lows of life with that football club. Although often severely tested, Brian's love for NUFC remains intact. Along the way, he has met countless fans, some of whom remain close friends to this day. Brian is divorced, and has three wonderful daughters, Claire, Kirsty, and Becky. Strangely enough, they too support Newcastle United Football Club. This is Brian's first book to be published, and he hopes to have more of his writings published in the future.

Editor/Publisher

Chris Foote Wood, an author in his own right, is one of Brian's many friends and also his writing partner. He has broadcast live radio reports on many United (and SAFC) games for the ILR (Independent Local Radio) network. Chris promised Brian he would publish his book in time for Christmas 2007 – it was originally planned to be out in August – but didn't reckon on Brian failing to deliver his final manuscript until well into November. But a promise is a promise, and with the help of some nifty footwork by printers Lintons of Crook, we just made it.

Chris modestly describes himself as author, editor, publisher, ghost-writer, broadcaster, voice-over artist, radio, tv & film scriptwriter and actor. His is currently helping Glenn McCrory, the only North-East boxer ever to be world champion, write his autobiography. Chris can be contacted on www.northernwriters.co.uk or www.writersinc.biz

Like this book?
Email your comments via www.writersinc.biz